George
Duke of Kent
1902-1942

Prince John
1905-1919

Gloucester

of Russia

=

ward Duke of Kent
5-

Alexandra
1936-

Prince Michael
1942-

=

James Ogilvy
1964-

Marina Ogilvy
1966-

# *Princess Alexandra*

# Princess Alexandra

Geoffrey Elborn

Sheldon Press · London

First published in Great Britain in 1982 by
Sheldon Press, SPCK, Marylebone Road, London NW1 4DU

British Library Cataloguing in Publication Data

Elborn, Geoffrey
  Princess Alexandra.
  1. Alexandra, *Princess*      2. Great Britain
  —Princes and princesses—Biography
  I. Title
  941.085'092'4        DA591.A3/
  ISBN 0-85969-376-7


Printed in Great Britain at The Camelot Press Ltd, Southampton

# Contents

*For my friends*
*Sacheverell Sitwell, and*
*Gertrude and Bernard Stevenson,*
*with my love and gratitude*

# INTRODUCTION

# *The Secret of Success*

THE PROSPECT OF meeting royalty throws most people into panic, even when the royal person is as kind and thoughtful as Princess Alexandra.

At an occasion when the present writer had been invited to see Princess Alexandra carrying out, for her, a routine engagement, the most level headed officials were darting about desperately trying to recall their instructions on etiquette and how to avoid any blunders.

In the event, Princess Alexandra arrived so quietly that some people in the packed room were unaware of her presence until she was suddenly amongst them, smiling and effortlessly asking questions; talking to those whom she had never met before, and knew very little about.

Although Princess Alexandra is sometimes considered a junior Princess and, in fact, is only twenty-first in line to the throne at the time of writing, her attendance at the function excited as much attention as The Queen would have created. The guests, emboldened by champagne soon nudged around each other in an effort to look at, and hopefully to be presented to, Princess Alexandra for the much desired accolade would be something to talk about later. Few think that they cannot be of the slightest interest to the Princess, but from Alexandra's obvious ease in conversation and her radiant smile, everyone who meets her leaves feeling important and somehow special. Many who meet Alexandra are so dazzled that they cannot recall what was spoken, only that she was so interested and kind.

When the present writer was presented to H.R.H. for the first time at such an engagement, she was quite clearly surprised that he should wish to write about her. As Princess Alexandra told the present writer,

I could understand if I was a great actress like Bernhardt, or a scientist like

vii

Marie Curie [pronounced in perfect French], then there would be something to write about. But I've done nothing. Why, only yesterday, I opened a turbine mill. What do I know about mills?

Princess Alexandra is genuinely modest, *and* interested in those she meets, and will go to great trouble to do her homework beforehand.

Perhaps she is happiest at musical events, for she attended the fiftieth birthday concert for the Master of the Queen's Music, Malcolm Williamson, in November 1981, and also the eightieth birthday concert for Sir William Walton in March 1982.

Malcolm Williamson, who had just returned from Tasmania, and is interested in helping the handicapped and disabled, had met a young blind musician who was exceptionally talented, and was in need of assistance to encourage and foster his talent. Despite the fact that the emphasis was on Mr Williamson's music, the Princess was at once interested in hearing about the musician, because of her work for the Royal Commonwealth Society for the Blind, and her Lady-in-Waiting was at hand to note down the details. Although there was a buffet for the guests in the reception room at the Royal Festival Hall, the Princess declined both food and alcohol, and chatted to the orchestra and choir.

Princess Alexandra's thoughtfulness expressed itself in a different way when she sat with Sir William Walton and his wife in the Royal Box for his birthday concert. She was unfailingly considerate about helping Sir William to his chair, and showed him various other kindnesses during a very joyful but emotional evening. When Sir William took ill a few days later and was in a London hospital, Princess Alexandra remembered her friend and sent flowers, with a hand written letter.

The Princess has never made any of the blunders which have occasionally been made by other members of her family, and has always displayed great patience under, what must be at times, very trying circumstances. She hardly ever seems to take any of her own feelings of tiredness into consideration. After a busy morning opening a girls' school in Colchester and talking to many pupils and teachers, she continued her engagements with a visit to Saffron Walden as part of the activities for the Year of the Disabled, in 1981. Several thousand handicapped people turned up, far more than expected, and they had to be put in a tatty disused hangar. Many had waited for hours to catch even a glimpse of the Princess and, despite the pouring rain, Alexandra wandered round at will, too quickly for her detective to follow her. One woman who caught a glimpse of the Princess was almost in tears, but perfectly happy. Her long vigil had been justified, for she declared, 'That's all I wanted to see'.

Despite Alexandra's apparent easy approachability, she is a very private person, and resents obvious efforts from those who mistake her sympathetic manner as an invitation to become familiar. During one reception she was presented with flowers, and showed no embarrassment when the speaker described her as Princess Margaret, and praised the bouquet which she handed Princess Alexandra. But when one man carried away with champagne said to her, 'You must come and have dinner with my wife,' she flickered her eyelids and, continuing to smile, asked instead if the unfortunate man had enjoyed the concert. When, through bad planning on the part of the organizing committee, she was obliged to meet everyone in the room, the Princess was not apparently perturbed, although even her skill in keeping instant conversation available must have been stretched. When she left the room finally, she did so without fuss, and without any sense of having to be elsewhere, although in fact, she had another engagement for which she was a little late.

The skill with which the Princess undertakes her functions, is justly famous, but was not acquired overnight. She has carried out thousands of duties since she first began as a young woman of seventeen in 1953, from beginnings which were unconventional by royal standards. From the start, however, Princess Alexandra has given all her duties a special touch which arose partly from her background, and partly from her personality.

During her first solo royal tour, in Australia, she invented the first royal walkabout. Now walkabouts are an accepted feature of royal programmes, but in 1959 it was an astonishing breakthrough that royalty could actually meet the people. Perhaps the idea could only have occurred to Alexandra, for she seemed determined from the outset of her public career to contribute *her* personal way of doing things. Rather than sticking to any expected or traditional patterns which other members of her family might have considered at least 'safe'.

Of course other members of her family do give enormous pleasure to the public they serve so well. Nevertheless it is often commented that there is something different about Princess Alexandra.

What is the secret of her success?

It is a question which produces at times surprising answers, for her life has been influenced by events and circumstances which have never before, or since, touched the concern of a British Princess.

# 1

# *Abdication Princess*

THE CHRISTMAS OF 1936 was a strained and eventful time for the royal family. Two weeks previously, the uncrowned king, Edward VIII, had abdicated the throne in order to marry Mrs Wallis Simpson, the final act of a drawn-out tragedy from which it would take years to recover. One of the most upset was Edward's brother, the Duke of Kent, who was present when the King made his farewell speech to the nation, and had been so shocked by the events that when the Duke of Windsor, as Edward became, bowed in homage to George VI he called out in despair, 'This isn't really happening.'

At the same time, the Duke of Kent was under additional stress; his wife was expecting a baby. So it was perhaps appropriate that Alexandra, as the baby was christened, chose no ordinary day to arrive. She was born on Christmas Day, a few weeks earlier than expected, and her appearance was more than welcome, for not only did it help to take the strain of recent events off the Duke of Kent's mind, and bring a little joy into his life, but it also seemed to establish a sense of stability in the monarchy, as far as the anxious public were concerned. From the beginning Alexandra was a notable public success.

Although Alexandra was expected in the New Year, her mother-to-be, Marina, the Duchess of Kent, had wisely decided not to join other members of the royal family on their traditional seasonal holiday at Sandringham. When it was clear that the Duchess's second baby was due, Marina remained in her Belgrave Square home, and the Home Secretary was hurriedly sent for, being at that time required to be present in the house when a royal birth was expected. Marina's parents, Prince and Princess Nicholas of Greece were also in Belgrave Square, and were slightly surprised when the waiting reporters were asked in by the Duke of Kent for a Christmas drink, a gesture typical of the family's openness and friendliness which Alexandra was to continue so notably.

If the Duke was nervous, nothing was allowed to break the usual routine of the house, at least where the young Prince Edward was concerned. He had been born only fifteen months earlier, and was old enough to enjoy being pushed in the pram by his nurse Miss Smith, and so off they went. Nanny Smith and the young Prince were out for their walk when someone called down stairs, 'It's a girl.' The baby was six and a half pounds, the birth had been quite straightforward, and both mother and daughter were well.

The Princess's birth heralded a reassuring start to the New Year, and indeed, when the news was brought to Queen Mary in her room at Sandringham, she remarked, 'The only nice thing to have happened this year.' From there, a message was sent to the King and Queen, who were attending morning service at the Sandringham Church. The news quickly leaked to the crowds, who greeted their monarch and his wife with extra loud cheers when the couple left the church.

The parents were delighted with their second baby, for Marina had hoped for a girl. She had managed to keep the news of her pregnancy well hidden, and might have done so for longer had not Queen Mary suggested a long rest of four months for her daughter-in-law. Once this decision was taken, nobody was in any doubt of the significance of the announcement that

H.R.H. The Duchess of Kent has cancelled her forthcoming engagements, and she will not be undertaking any further functions.

So the nation's thoughts were with Marina. But it had not always been so. In her comfortable home in London's fashionable Belgrave Square, few would have guessed that the beautiful Greek Princess who had married the handsome Prince George, had endured an extremely unsettled and difficult early life.

The grand-daughter of the first King of Greece, Marina, born in 1906, lived for the early part of her childhood in Athens with her parents, Prince Nicholas and his Russian-born wife, Princess Helen. But the King was assassinated, the republicans gained control, and the Greek Royal family were forced into exile in Switzerland. After a brief return to Athens, it was not long before Marina and her family were obliged to leave Greece, this time for good, and live in Paris. The royal family were forbidden to return to their home country, and all their property was confiscated.

The situation would have been depressing for anyone less practical than Marina's parents. However, they were realistic about their circumstances, and Prince Nicholas, who was a good amateur painter, helped boost his rather meagre income by the sale of some of his works. Marina, who was only fifteen when her family moved to France, was educated at a Paris boarding school, and there learnt many languages, including English. Her family often used to visit England, and especially favoured some of the seaside resorts, such as Bognor Regis, much loved by George V. Marina, would often be accompanied by her Nurse, Miss Fox, who had helped Marina with her English. 'Foxy' was a kind but strict companion who nevertheless encouraged Marina to develop her talent of mimicry, as well as her great gift for painting, which she had inherited from her father.

When in England, in 1934, Marina and her parents were invited to dinner with Emerald, Lady Cunard, the famous London society hostess. Amongst the guests was Prince George, the younger son of George V. He was always known as 'PG' and his good looks made him popular company, adding to the notoriety gained from his high-spirited involvement with what was described as 'fast society'. No one was more anxious than Queen Mary that George should settle down and marry, but he had shown little inclination to do this. After a brief career in the Navy, which he had not enjoyed, George had taken Civil Service exams as a Factory Inspector. At Lady Cunard's dinner, he told Marina about his experiences, and the two spent a considerable time chatting.

He was quite entranced with Marina, and arranged to see her the following evening at Claridges Hotel. Prince Paul, Marina's brother-in-law, suspecting that the couple were becoming fond of each other, invited George to spend a short holiday with him at Bohinji in Yugoslavia, and he privately arranged for Marina to be there also. After five days, George proposed to Marina, and they were engaged on 21 August 1934.

Queen Mary and King George were only too happy to give their consent to the marriage, for they had long thought that only after marriage would George really settle down. He had shocked his own family by taking girlfriends openly to the cinema, and surprised even his brother Edward VIII, himself no prude, with his rather reckless behaviour in public. Despite all this, he was ideally suited to Marina, for like her, he had a love of the arts, played the piano well, and had inherited from his mother a great love and knowledge of antiques. The gruff George V glowed with pleasure when he met Marina, and confided in his diary, 'Marina was looking very pretty and charming, and will be a great addition to the family. . . .'

The engagement was made public on 28 August 1934, but the cautious British public were less than enthusiastic, being suspicious of a foreign princess of whom they knew nothing, and feeling that the popular George should have married a princess from his own country, or at least someone they knew about. The Press were equally surprised. Marina was so unknown that there was no photograph of her to publish with the announcement, and one had to be expressed from Paris.

However, all the opposition to Marina disappeared when the story of the early struggles of her family became public. When it was pointed out that their own much loved Queen Alexandra, from whom Marina was descended, was herself a princess 'from over the sea', the British public were delighted, and ready to appreciate her beauty and charm. By the time she arrived from Paris at Folkestone, feelings had altered so much that she was greeted by a ceremonial band and, at Victoria Station when she left for Buckingham Palace, flowers were even thrown in front of her car, one of the last occasions when this special tribute was ever paid to anyone.

Preparations for the wedding cheered a country beset by growing unemployment. Marina was conscious of the poverty of the working classes, and in a gesture quite unprecedented by any member of the royal family, announced that she would

like the people of England [sic] to share in some way my great happiness on the occasion of my engagement to Prince George. As you know, my years of exile have taught me how much unhappiness there is in the world. Although I should be happy to think that the preparations for my wedding were in some small measure giving employment to those who need it, I should be more than happy for the unemployed and particularly their children, to receive any money which has been intended for the purpose of wedding gifts . . .

It was a decision that Marina had made with Prince George, and by way of a side-effect, guaranteed her lasting popularity in Britain.

The Kents' wedding, the first royal marriage to be broadcast on the wireless, took place on the frosty morning of 29 November 1934. Marina drove to Westminster Abbey in a state landau. Her silver and brocade gown, incorporating the English rose in its design, had been worked by Russian refugees, at Marina's request.

After her honeymoon, Marina was thrown into the rounds of duties undertaken by any new member of the royal family, but it was not to

last for long. Ten months after her marriage, Marina, now Duchess of
Kent, gave birth to her first child, Prince Edward, on 9 October 1935.

He had been christened in the chapel in Buckingham Palace, and it
was there that he went over a year later to watch the baptism of his
sister, the six-week-old Princess Alexandra, in February 1937. It had
been a busy day for the King, who had held the first levee of his reign at
St James's Palace that morning, before lunching with the Kents at
Belgrave Square.

Many of Marina's relatives from abroad were also present at the
Christening, perhaps most remarkably, the elderly Princess Louise of
Argyle, Queen Victoria's fourth daughter, who had herself been
christened in the chapel in 1848. Alexandra Helen Elizabeth Olga
Christabel – all names from Marina's family, except the last, which
reflected the Princess's birthday on 25 December – was the last baby to
be christened in the chapel, for four years later enemy bombs were to
destroy it.

The infant Princess wore the traditional Honiton lace robe, and cried
loudly during the ceremony, something which also inspired her brother
to tears. But with the calming presence of the King and Queen
Elizabeth, as god parents, all was well. There had been some anxious
moments when Alexandra, with a strength of character that would
later become all too apparent, tried to thrust away the arm of the
Archbishop of Canterbury as he anointed her forehead with the water
from the River Jordan.

Later that evening, the Duke and Duchess of Kent attended a dance
in the Dorchester Hotel, leaving the princess in the capable hands of
Nurse Smith, and a few days after the christening the couple left for a
six-week holiday, before returning for the coronation preparations in
May. But it was not long before Alexandra was again in the public eye,
this time under the dramatic circumstances of a 'Royal Motor
Accident'.

The Duchess was driving to Sandwich in Kent, with Prince Edward
and Alexandra, when the chauffeur-driven car was involved in a
collision. All the side windows were smashed, and fragments of glass
covered the cot in which Alexandra lay. When it was lifted out of the
car, the Princess was found to be completely unharmed, but it had been
a very near miss. While the family waited for a relief car to arrive, it was
discovered that Marina had lost her engagement ring. Although a
search was carried out, it was unsuccessful, and Marina had to

continue the journey without it, the ring finally being found several days later.

The shaken Kents continued to Bloody House Point, an attractive stretch of sands. Marina, who had so often enjoyed the pleasures of the English seaside, was determined that her own children should enjoy them as she had.

# 2

# *Wartime Childhood*

ALEXANDRA GREW UP in the house where she was born, 3 Belgrave Square, at the centre of Belgravia, the fashionable and wealthy area near Buckingham Palace. The Kents had leased the house when they were married from Lady Juliet Duff, a famous society hostess, and had quickly made it their own home. Marina, scorning the sharp geometric lines of the age's more fashionable salons, dictated the colour scheme of 'off-whites', and left the choice of furnishings to her husband. Before very long, they were established in a comfortable family home, and no room was more traditional than the children's nursery, in blue and white, with an attractive rug covered with pictures illustrating nursery rhymes.

Prince Edward, even as a small boy, was fascinated by anything mechanical, an interest he inherited from his father. He would gladly take his toys to pieces, and then reassemble them, and when he was older he would often help his father in the garage, carrying out small repair jobs on the family car. His practical interests drew him close to Prince George, who adored his son. Marina too was devoted to her children, and spent as much time as she could with them, often wheeling Alexandra in her pram in Hyde Park and nearby. Nanny Smith, who had looked after Marina's nephews and nieces in Yugoslavia, proved to be the ideal governess, for although strict, she ensured that everything in the home ran smoothly. Alexandra learnt as she grew older that she was not to annoy the servants, and Nanny Smith informed them that they were to leave her in peace to enjoy a normal childhood, without undue fuss.

When Miss Smith had her day off, old Miss Fox, Marina's own nanny, now officially retired and living in Hampstead, would come to Belgrave Square to help out. Her authority was supreme, and she would often stay at Belgrave Square when the Kents were absent abroad. Marina missed the company of her family, and George, who adored travelling, was always delighted to take his wife to Paris or Yugoslavia for a reunion.

At home, the Kents carried out their duties with informed interest, and their hosts soon learned to expect more than smiling and waving. The Duke's experience from his studies in the Civil Service proved invaluable when he was touring the depressed industrial North of England. With his expert knowledge of factories, he would talk to the workers on their own terms, not his, and meet the unemployed, while Marina always had time to talk with the poor and their children with sympathy and understanding.

While on such a tour on Merseyside the Kents were as usual invited to attend many dinners and receptions. But overwhelmed by the bleakness of what they had seen, Marina and George refused to attend most of them, for they felt it was morally wrong to enjoy such luxuries when so many they had seen and met were starving. Instead, they arranged to give an informal tea party for the widows and relatives of the victims of a recent submarine disaster. The Kents met the unhappy people in a reception room at Liverpool airport, and while Marina talked to the women, the Duke played with their children and repaired some of their broken toys. It was a memorable and a genuinely comforting day for their guests, and a gesture typical of the simple kindness and warmth of the Kents.

Marina had acquired this inherent sympathy from her mother, Princess Helen, who had opened a home in Paris for Russian refugees with money raised from selling jewels she had smuggled out of Athens. It was then that Marina, who relied on the help of English friends to raise more funds for the home remarked,

It is the poor who help the most, especially the English people. They are so kind. Once you have gained their friendship, they never let you down.

Marina saw this at first hand in England, but did more than merely offer sympathy and took practical steps to encourage industry in areas where production was at a low ebb, and thousands were unemployed. As a member of the royal family, she could not intervene directly in political matters or in business, but she was well aware how she influenced fashion, and when she heard of the desperate state of slump in the Lancashire cotton mills, she hit on a practical way of helping. For a whole summer, Marina wore various dresses of cotton print then considered worthy only of the working class, and certainly not to be seen on anyone in society. As expected, her dresses started a new fashion, and the increased demand for cotton prints inspired competition and resulted in more work for the cotton mills and better quality goods.

This iron will of Marina's would also influence her children, although sometimes their father would take charge. As Edward and Alexandra grew the family moved out of London to a new house called Coppins, near Iver in Buckinghamshire. The house had belonged to Princess Victoria, the youngest daughter of Edward VII, who, realizing that the Kents were not particularly well off, had left them the house when she died in 1936.

Coppins was rather an ugly house, built in the 1850s for John Mitchell, who had held Queen Victoria's Royal Warrrant as a theatre and concert agent. The red brick walls were draped in heavy ivy, and the rooms inside were filled with Edwardian bric à brac and overcrowded with heavy furniture. Nevertheless, it had many possibilities, and its greatest immediate attraction was that it would provide more room for the children than had the house in Belgrave Square, including a large nursery.

Marina and George removed most of the old furnishings, and, as at Belgrave Square, George led the way. A family friend noted

He had very definite ideas about furniture and decoration . . . . He practically ran the house and dictated its decoration. She was entirely dominated by him – and adored him. He collected very lovely furniture, and filled Coppins with chintzes and lightened its atmosphere, inside and out . . . .

Only a small staff were kept at Coppins: a footman who also doubled as a butler, two chauffeurs, a cook and a few maids. If there was any shirking of duty in the kitchens, the housekeeper had only to look up to be reminded of her royal duty by stern looks from a portrait of Queen Victoria which hung in her room.

The great advantage of Coppins for Alexandra and Edward was the large nursery, which opened on to the spacious lawns. At first, enthusiastic passers-by were able to see over the brick wall to where Alexandra played, and a large fence had to be constructed to keep out their inquisitive gaze. It was just as well, for Queen Mary was a frequent guest at Coppins, and would have been even more upset by outside stares than would the children. Queen Mary had become very fond of her grand-daughter, for she found life more lonely than her regality would ever allow her to admit. She was close to her son, with whom she could talk about her beloved antiques, and George was always happy to receive advice from Queen Mary about improvements to the house.

It was a contented family life that Queen Mary saw, but in fact, although the Kents were very much in love with each other, the early years of their marriage were not always easy. Both had strong personalities, and were used to different kinds of freedom. Marina could not accustom herself to some of the strictures of the Court, and found it difficult at times to accept her new life. George wished to dominate the marriage, and was often moody when he met with Marina's opposition. He found it hard to break away from his bachelor friends, whom he often missed, and friends often felt that, devoted to Marina as he was, he was not the marrying kind of a man. There were suggestions that he had been pressed into marrying Marina too early, to please Queen Mary.

This said, many of the problems the Kents had to cope with were quite understandable, Marina was really a stranger in a foreign country, and at times felt alone, with few friends of her own. To compensate for her feeling of isolation, she would make long telephone calls to either Paris or Yugoslavia, the expense of which infuriated her husband. Neither did the Duke care for Miss Fox, and he felt that her influence was excessive. He tried to have her removed, but Marina refused, and by her contrivance the old nurse would always try to visit the household when she knew that the Duke was not there.

When there was a sense of strain, Marina would play with the children, and George would moodily relax at the piano, but the problems did not last, for the Kents were drawn together by their mutual love of the children, and by the time that war came, the couple were unreservedly devoted to each other.

Even so, there were still times when it seemed that the moody atmosphere affected the children, and especially the young and impressionable Alexandra. It was noticed that she was shy and difficult with guests, and would refuse to shake hands with them. Sometimes when she was asked to leave the room, she would refuse to do so, and would instead lie wriggling and protesting in a cross voice on the floor. George rarely interfered with his daughter's behaviour, and normally left her discipline to Marina, although on one occasion when she kicked over a fully laden tea-trolley, she was promptly smacked by her father.

Alexandra's behaviour was no more difficult than many other children of her age, and it would be a mistake to suggest that it was any more serious than simply part of the process of growing up. It is important to remember, though, that at times it must have been confusing for children of families such as Alexandra's, who had to learn to receive a variety of affection from both her nurse and her mother. To make matters worse, Marina and her husband were often obliged to be away from their home for lengthy periods. Many children from this sort of family fared worse than Edward and Alexandra, and grew more attached to the nanny who looked after them than their own parents, whom they saw less often.

Meanwhile, the growing threat of war seemed to dwindle, for a while at least. The Duke of Kent was himself in the public gallery of the House of Commons to hear Chamberlain, newly returned from Munich, confidently declare that the war had been averted and that there would be 'peace in our time'. George felt reassured enough to continue with his plans for the departure to Australia, for he had been appointed Governor-General designate of that country, and was due to start his term of office in 1939.

It was an exciting time for the Kents and their children, with much to be done. Furniture was already on its way to Australia, and the family discussed with a feeling of excitement the plans for their new house, and the requirements for Alexandra and Edward's nursery. Although it was an upheaval, and Marina would be even further away from her family, Australia offered an exciting challenge.

As part of the preparations for the visit, the photographer Baron arrived at Coppins to take publicity shots of the family. An idea of a certain formality that Marina liked on such occasions can be inferred from the results, which seem strangely inappropriate even for British children of that time, and certainly for the more relaxed Australia for which the photographs were intended. Edward, in particular, looked unnatural, dressed rather stiffly in a silk suit that might have been worn at a royal wedding. Marina, it seemed, was still very much influenced by her strict upbringing and had definite ideas of the image she wished to present to the world of her children. Fortunately, Alexandra, at two and a half, was too young for such formal clothes, and instead wore a simple embroidered dress. Her lively behaviour must have been agony for her mother, though, for the young Princess refused to stay still in any pose. The prints show her lying back on a couch, displaying chubby legs, and laughing happily with a smile that was anything but regal. Perhaps someone pointed out to Marina afterwards how 'posed' some of the photographs of Edward looked, and how charming was the buoyant Alexandra, for later shots of her children were utterly different, with Edward and Alexandra in dungarees.

In the event, all plans for Australia had to be cancelled, as it became clear that Britain would once again be involved in a war with Germany. Instead, Marina and George went for a long cruise in the Aegean in the summer of 1939, and while they were away, their children stayed at Sandringham with Queen Mary who, since, the death of George V, had delighted in the company of her grandchildren, and that summer she would happily busy herself with her needlework while Alexandra and Edward played nearby.

As the European crisis reached its peak, the Kents were forced to return to Britain. It was a difficult time for Marina, for she had seen her mother in Athens. Since the death of her husband, Prince Nicholas, in 1938, Princess Helen had been left alone, and Marina wondered just when she would see her mother again. Family loyalties were also strained, because of the political situation, as the three daughters of Marina's cousin, Princess Andrew, sisters of the present Duke of Edinburgh, had all married German officers.

More immediately, however, Marina and George were worried about the safety of their own children, and they travelled to Sandringham to discuss the problem with other members of the royal family, who met there on 25 August. It was agreed that if war broke out, Queen Mary would leave her home in Malborough House in London, and stay at Badminton in Gloucestershire with her niece the Duchess of Beaufort, and her husband the Duke, who was always known as 'Master'. As Coppins was considered a likely target for German bombers, and was near London, it was also decided that the two Kent children would stay at Badminton.

Chamberlain's announcement of the declaration of war on 3 September confirmed the arrangements. The Kents gave up the lease of their Belgrave Square home, and for some time took a house at Tetbury, in Gloucestershire, not far from Badminton.

Alexandra and Edward were with Queen Mary at Sandringham on the day war was declared, and in the early hours of the next day, 4 September, 'an air raid signal at 2.45 drove us from our beds', as Queen Mary wrote in her diary. Queen Mary, always dignified, refused to hurry, and dressed at her usual pace while her detective waited outside her room. She arrived in the basement of the house where the staff had gathered for safety, and found that Alexandra and Edward '. . . were there and behaved beautifully. At 3.30 we heard the "All clear" so I returned to bed but not to sleep.'

Despite the unsettled night, Queen Mary left with the little prince and princess later that morning. 'My servants & luggage followed my cars – quite a fleet', Queen Mary recorded in her diary. In fact, a huge procession of over twenty cars and luggage vans, with nearly a hundred staff, made their way, to Gloucestershire. They stopped for luncheon at Althorp, the Spencer seat, where Alexandra and Edward enjoyed a rice pudding as part of the meal.

It was early evening when the convoy finally arrived, and it was not until a few days later that Marina visited her children. She found that they had settled in very well, for as Queen Mary remarked, 'I've adopted the house and the family as my own.'

Indeed, Queen Mary involved her grandchildren in many of her own activities. If the weather was poor, Alexandra and Edward would play in the nursery, while someone would read to the Queen, but if the day was warm and sunny, Queen Mary would drive with the Kent children in a farmworker's cart, to save petrol, and they would make for groups of trees covered with ivy. The party would scramble out and tug the offending creeper clear of the trunks. The Dowager Queen had a fixation about removing ivy, and no derelict building was safe from her attack, but it was not a pastime that Marina and George were pleased to hear about. The King had remarked, 'Queen Mary once gave me and Lilibet (the present Queen) ivy poisoning, by making us pick it off walls at Sandringham.'

Happier and more fruitful expeditions were those organized by Queen Mary to gather old petrol cans and scrap metal for the war effort. The old lady's energy was quite remarkable, and she encouraged her grandchildren to work with a group of Birmingham evacuees, and to pile the 'rubbish' into wheelbarrows. It is doubtful whether Alexandra could have helped much at three and a half, but undoubtedly she enjoyed the excitement. It was, too, a confusing time for such a small child, for although Queen Mary had a reputation for being stiff and formal, she seemed to relax with children that were not her own. The reputation was not ill-founded; at Buckingham Palace, when her husband was King, her sons had been made to bow to their parents as they took leave of them each evening.

But it was different at Badminton. During a dance there, Queen Mary grabbed a small boy and whirled him into a lively waltz. 'Never forget,' she told him, 'that you've danced with an old lady of seventy-seven.' It was Queen Mary who brought a sense of calm during the most terrifying moments at Badminton, when she was forced to retreat to a shelter for safety, taking with her the Kent children amongst others. Remaining fully dressed and alert, Queen Mary watched over the sleeping children, who were wrapped in blankets, until it was safe to return to the house. The old queen was quite unperturbed by any threat of danger, and would pass the time doing the crossword in her newspaper.

In London, meantime, the Duchess of Kent had taken a job as an auxiliary nurse at University College Hospital. Marina was anxious that her royal status should not hinder her work there, and kept her identity a secret from everyone except the hospital officials. Known as 'Nurse K' it was assumed that her name was Kay and for a time nobody guessed who she was. At one point, Marina was even lined up with the rest of the staff to be presented to the Duke of Kent, who was inspecting the hospital in his capacity as President. Marina curtseyed with great skill, but managed to keep her face quite expressionless, and George also betrayed no sign of recognition. Eventually, several patients were certain that they recognized the Duchess in their helpful and kindly nurse, and one told the press.

It was an exhausting time for Marina, for when she was not at the hospital she was still carrying out her official engagements, which were more important than ever. Often she would travel over three hundred miles a week, visiting factories, bombed areas and centres for vital war work. Marina put her country first, and although she was often dropping from fatigue, she knew how much a friendly smile and a kind word meant to those who were working night and day to prevent the threat of Nazi invasion in Britain. She must also have felt rather lonely. The war severely disrupted Marina's family life, for George was stationed for a while as Rear-Admiral at the naval base in Rosyth in Scotland.

After Bath was bombed, in 1941, Alexandra and Edward returned to Coppins for a while, because it was thought to be safer. It was a wonderfully happy time for the family, reunited after a lengthy spell of disruption. All the early domestic difficulties had gone, and Marina and George spent much of the time improving the garden.

Alexandra was later remembered by Lady Colville, one of the Women of the Bedchamber of Queen Mary's Household, who saw the small Princess during harvest time. Wearing a blue frock and a straw hat '. . . the reins in her hand, feeling entirely responsible for the dignified progress of the bulging crop . . . she made a delightful figure as a rural driver, and was as brave as a lion. . . .' There was an informal atmosphere during those years of Alexandra's childhood. Friends of the Duke and Duchess took a small house called Coppins Cottage, and would often call with visitors. When both George and Marina were there they also held some small dinner parties. Their friend Baroness de Stoeckl, remembered that Marina looked:

. . . a dream in an evening gown – always punctual. He would come in a little late, looking so sleek, so *soigné*, so good looking. We could have a cocktail, and walk into the dining room, the only light was from four long candles on the table. The food on the sideboard was kept hot by electric heaters. He was so graceful, so tall, fair and slim. He usually served me, then the others would help themselves, he always last. Everything was perfect. He used to give orders for such-and-such a centre-piece to be put on the table. I used to forget half the time to remark on the beauty of it, but the Duchess would make me a sign and I would be loud in my admiration. He would be so pleased. We used to sit at the table until a quarter to eleven o'clock. I would long to get up, but that was his special hour of relaxation. He would talk and discuss and drink several cups of coffee. When many guests were present, then the servants served. After dinner we used to walk towards the music room. After a few minutes he would seat himself before one of the pianos and play endlessly . . .

The happy domestic life at Coppins was complete when Marina gave birth to her second son, Michael, on 4 July 1942. Alexandra and Edward were brought back from Badminton, to which they had returned, to see their new brother, and one month later they went with their parents to Windsor Chapel for the christening. Because of the war, the Kents had decided that the ceremony would be a private one, with only the royal family and some of the Coppins staff present.

It was to be the last occasion when the Duke was in the company of so many of his family. During the days that followed at Coppins, he showed a tender devotion to his youngest son, and even after a busy day would silently watch the child asleep in his cot in the nursery.

There was nothing to suggest the terrible tragedy that was to follow. The Duke was due to fly to Iceland from Invergordon in Scotland, where he would inspect the troops before leaving. The first stage of his journey to Scotland was to be made by car, but before he set off in the late afternoon of 24 August, he found time to do a little gardening with his wife.

Baroness de Stoeckl had been organizing a fête, and was puzzled by the Duke's refusal to commit himself to be there. Mysteriously as the Duke was saying his farewells to his family and friends, he turned to his butler, who was holding the Duke's favourite chow dog, and remarked, 'What will you do with him when I am gone?'

The following evening, Marina went to bed early. Soon after, the telephone rang from Balmoral, where the King and Queen were staying, to be answered by Miss Fox, the Duchess's oldest friend. She had been with Marina through the hard early years of her life, and now it fell on her to convey the saddest message of all to her mistress. The Duke of Kent had been killed when his plane crashed into a hill in Scotland.

An elderly crofter and his son had been out looking for sheep in the mist in the Morven Hills, when they had heard the low roar of a plane, and then a loud crash. The son ran to raise the alert, and the rescue party which was quickly gathered together was hampered by poor weather, and had to abandon the search when darkness fell. The following day, at noon, the police, shepherds and crofters who had formed the search party saw smoke rising in the distance, and were led to a heap of scattered wreckage. Lying in the heather were several bodies, including that of the Duke of Kent and his secretary. Only one man had survived. He had dragged the bodies from the plane before it exploded, and then staggered through the night, looking for help.

Marina was overwhelmed with grief when she heard the news. Alexandra and Edward were staying at Sandringham and were not told until later when they returned to Coppins. For Queen Mary, the death of her beloved George left her very shaken. 'I felt so stunned by the shock I could not believe it,' she wrote in her diary. It had only been a few weeks since Queen Mary had visited the Kents at Coppins, and had written with great pleasure of her son;' he looked so happy with his lovely wife & the dear baby.' But Queen Mary, who had seen so many family deaths and had borne them all with great fortitude, thought only of Marina, well aware of how desolate her daughter-in-law would be feeling. Queen Mary told Lady Cynthia Colville, 'I must go to Marina tomorrow.'

Marina was indeed desolate. She was unable to control fits of weeping, and at other times, would stare out of the window, unable to talk to anyone, or go to meals. The King thoughtfully arranged for her sister Princess Olga to come to stay with Marina, and for Queen Mary to pay periodic visits. It was decided that Alexandra and Edward should return to Gloucestershire, for there was still the ordeal of the funeral.

When it seemed that Marina would break down during the funeral service in St George's Chapel, Windsor, it was the Queen, now Queen Elizabeth the Queen Mother, who tenderly grasped her arm to give her reassurance, something she would do for the Duchess of Windsor thirty years later in the same place, despite her dislike for the woman who had so affected their lives. George VI was overcome with sadness, and noted

I have attended very many family funerals in the Chapel, but none . . . which have moved me in the same way. Everbody there I knew well, but I did not dare to look at any of them for the fear of breaking down.

To a friend, the King confided that he would miss his brother terribly. 'Thank God, he didn't suffer pain. I feel so desperately sorry for Marina . . . . Her life was entirely bound up with his . . .'

Confused, and bitterly lonely, Marina was finding it difficult to recreate a new life for herself. Kind but firm advice from Queen Mary, however, gradually took effect. She told her daughter-in-law that for the sake of her children, Marina must pick up the threads and carry on. And bravely, Marina tried.

It was a process that would take many months, however, even though the Duchess threw herself into her duties with great energy. Her friends often wrote to officials of functions Marina was due to attend, warning them not to refer to the late Duke in speeches, or privately to his widow, for Marina was liable to break down at the mention of the Duke's name, or if she saw a photograph of him.

Alexandra remained with Queen Mary for the rest of the war, and for special treats, would be driven in Queen Mary's car, seated next to her grandmother, while clutching her favourite doll Christabel. Eventually, when the danger was over, the family were reunited, and nobody welcomed the return of Alexandra and Edward to Coppins more than Marina. Only her children could comfort her now, and it was largely due to them that Marina found the courage to continue.

# 3

# *High Spirits*

MARINA WAS SLOWLY finding that she was liked for herself, and not just, as she had once feared, because she was the Duke of Kent's wife, and the affection the public showed towards Marina helped her to gain confidence, and to appreciate life as far as was possible without her husband. It was a tremendous relief that the war was over, and Marina became totally absorbed in her baby son, and cheered by the lively Alexandra and her elder brother. Both children had a tremendous sense of fun, and in their company it was impossible to feel miserable for long.

Queen Mary became a more frequent visitor to Coppins, for she found in Marina a woman with the same sense of purpose and dedication to public life as herself. Although completely different in taste, both women shared strong views on fashion. Queen Mary had never varied her style of dress, and her only attempt to shorten the length of her skirt had been frowned upon by her husband. Queen Mary admired the elegant Marina who never faltered in keeping her faultless appearance.

The children were always smart, setting an example to the village, where they would be allowed to buy sweets with their coupons from the local shop in Iver. On one occasion, when Queen Mary was staying with them, the Queen noticed Edward looking rather sad when Edward and Alexandra returned from such an expedition. She asked her grandson what was troubling him, and he told her, 'Rising prices.'

Rising prices not only worried Edward, but also Marina. With her husband's death his Civil List annuity had ceased, and Parliament had not voted any income for his widow. Marina refused to draw the war widow's pension to which she was entitled, but instead, she was obliged to sell some of the house's objets d'art to raise capital. For some years, the Kents would feel the strain of frugal living. Royalty were subject to the same clothing coupon restrictions as everyone else, and it was noticed that Alexandra was often photographed in clothes which had been worn by her cousins, Princess Elizabeth and Princess Margaret. Alexandra would find this embarrassing, especially when other children recognized it. But complaining would do no good, Marina was perhaps at times over conscientious in her duties as a single parent, but she was not worried about financial hardship. After all, she herself had not suffered adversely in the long run from a similar lack of luxury during her childhood. She was soon proved right. Alexandra could not be miserable for long. A visitor to Coppins noticed that Alexandra struck her as . . .

. . . being very pretty and extraordinarily lively, attractively mischievous, with the brightest eyes I have ever seen. She got on admirably with her grandmother Queen Mary, who was at moments taken aback by her energy, but fascinated too, and who bore her grand-daughter's exuberance with amused fortitude. . . .

Queen Mary was possibly absent when Alexandra went through a rather embarrassing 'horsey' phase, taking matters a little further than most. She would refuse to eat her food unless it resembled oats, declaring that she must grow to be a strong horse. Conversation was restricted to loud whinnying and neighing, which visitors found amusing, but which did not please Marina. As small consolation, Alexandra's enthusiasm brought the reward of a prize for the best groomed pony at a local show when she was eight, but even that was not above suspicion – the bright gloss on the animal's coat was achieved by a large bottle of her mother's brilliantine.

Alexandra was inclined to tomboy ways, being often led on in pranks and escapades by her brother Edward.

For some time, both the young Kent children were educated locally, in a house called York Cottage. Run by a pleasant teacher named Mrs Parnell, Alexandra and Edward shared their class with the doctor's sons. Alexandra received private lessons in dancing, and in music. She was to become a particularly fine pianist, a gift she inherited from her father, and one which would please Marina, who although she enjoyed listening to music, played no instrument herself.

Those early years at Coppins, where the young Alexandra mixed with some of the local children, were to be an important influence on her attitude to other social classes, and her gift of being undoubtedly one of the best mixers of the royal family.

Yet Alexandra's skill in this direction must have surprised Marina, for at times she was even a little shocked by Alexandra's behaviour, and the contradictions in her young daughter's character. One friend recalled that the Princess was

> an impossible little girl. If she didn't get her own way, you know, she would go puce in the face and scream the place down. I've seen such rages. . . . She would smash toys, rush about all over the place, and even try to push over furniture. She was a real terror, who would refuse to go to bed, and would hide instead in the garden. . . .

Marina was torn between her sense of duty as a mother and her devotion to her daughter. She herself had the same strong sense of independence as her daughter, although when Alexandra's age she expressed it in different ways. Marina knew too, that in time Alexandra would grow out of her problems, and although when severely tried, she would complain 'I just don't know what to do with Alexandra! She's the very limit', Marina wisely felt that her daughter '. . . must have a chance to grow up quietly like any other girl.'

It was a sensible ambition, but one which not unnaturally brought problems. Alexandra was not like any other girl, she was a princess. Marina had to try to instill in Alexandra an awareness of her daughter's special position without letting it suggest any particular advantage or privilege. Alexandra was helped to a large extent by her experience at Badminton, and also by the rather informal schooling in the village. Of course, her school friends were selected for her, but Alexandra could make trips to the local shops, to watch the butcher making sausages, and although an apparently trivial experience, it was a breakthrough for a member of the royal family.

It is said that Alexandra at times found it difficult which identity to assume; whether to be a princess, or simply an ordinary girl. For any young child, it would be disturbing to be told one minute that 'you are a princess', and the next to be warned not to feel superior because of it.

A story is told that when Alexandra was eleven, and being driven to Ballater near Balmoral by the chauffeur Nutbeam, the Princess waved a little too enthusiastically to the cheering crowds who lined the streets. Her flamboyant display embarrassed Edward, who slid down on to the car floor to avoid being seen. When it was explained to Alexandra that she should be a little more restrained, she is alleged to have replied rather grandly, 'Why shouldn't I wave, after all I am a Princess and it is expected of me to wave to my people!' Marina's advice that royalty were there to serve, for all their special position, was difficult for the high-spirited girl to remember.

Eventually something was done. Alexandra found it hard to contain her excitement when she learned that she was to be a bridesmaid at the wedding of Lord Mountbatten's daughter, Patricia, to Lord Brabourne. Alexandra's charming appearance of innocence, crowned by a floral tiara, did not go unobserved by the King and Queen, but, neither did her slightly boisterous behaviour at the wedding breakfast. George VI felt partly responsible for the welfare of his niece, because of the death of his brother, the Duke of Kent. After a family conference, the Duchess of Gloucester suggested a governess for Alexandra, and the shaping of a princess began.

# 4

# *Heathfield*

MISS PEEBLES, A Scot in her early twenties, was perhaps, to be the inspiration of the gradual emergence into public life which was to be Alexandra's inevitable path in the years following the war. 'Bambi', as Alexandra quickly christened the new governess because of her large brown eyes, must have found it an equally exciting time; she was a newcomer to royalty, although her credentials included periods of looking after a daughter of a Lady-in-Waiting to the Duchess of Gloucester, and also Susanna Cross, who later married Francis Sitwell, younger son of the poet and writer Sacheverell. Nevertheless, she was not distracted from her profession's ideal of 'fairness and firmness', and it was under just such a régime that the young princess flourished. At the side of Miss Peebles, who became an instant success in the Kent household, the effervescent Alexandra learned to control her lively spirits on even the most exciting occasions, such as the frequent visits to the zoo or boat trips down the Thames.

When the King heard of the progress his niece had made, he invited Alexandra to join the royal family at Ascot. As it happened, Alexandra was not impressed by what she saw, except perhaps by the strawberries and cream , and apparently she was bored by having to stand around looking pleasant. But if Ascot was dreary, it was a significant step forward. The young princess had faced the celebrity's particular problem of being on display before people she did not know. The next step was even more momentous for one in her situation. It was decided by the King that Alexandra should prepare to go to school.

For a British princess even to be considered for school was a remarkable step, and quite unprecedented in the royal family. George VI would perhaps have made the same decision for his daughters had the war not intervened, but now that it was over he was anxious that Alexandra should break away from the tradition of nannies and governesses. Miss Peebles had given Alexandra a thorough grounding in English, History and Music, and a tutor was brought in to help her with her Mathematics, still rather weak. In the meantime, Marina began the search for a suitable school for her daughter.

But before this step into uniformity, Alexandra was blossoming as a public figure. Earlier in 1947 Queen Mary took Alexandra, Princess Marina, and the Duke and Duchess of Gloucester to the British Industries Fair at the Olympia Exhibition Hall. Alexandra shyly held onto her mother's hand as demure as any parent could wish, until they reached the toy section. There, while dutifully examining the games at various stalls, she was told by one exhibitor to choose a present for herself. Ignoring Marina's suggestion of a small toy cat, Alexandra instead selected from a display feature a large cat of about her own size, clearly not on offer, but a choice which delighted the onlookers. Reluctantly, Alexandra was persuaded to accept a small painted dog. With this one piece of childish charm, Alexandra had captivated the public, but it was reported that Queen Mary was not pleased by the space given to the incident by the press, nor by being so unexpectedly upstaged.

Meanwhile, schools were still being surveyed to receive the princess. Certain obvious choices were rejected, such as Benenden, and Cheltenham Ladies' College, as Marina was more interested in reports she had heard of Heathfield School, near Ascot, then run by a Miss Kathleen Dodds, the youngest public school headmistress in the country. In fact, reports of Heathfield were not universally favourable: Alexandra's Yugoslavian cousin and namesake had been there before the war, and had hated it, eventually going on hunger strike until she was taken away. More recently though, the resolution of Miss Dodds, who had been appointed in 1945, had done much to improve conditions and morale at the school. Tina Onassis had enjoyed it, as had more importantly one of Alexandra's closest friends, Lady Diana Herbert, who had been at the school for a few terms already and was very hopeful that Alexandra would join her there. The school had no Common Entrance Exam, another point in its favour in the eyes of Marina, who was slightly doubtful of her daughter's scholastic ability. After a meeting with Miss Dodds, it was decided that Alexandra would join the school in the Spring Term of 1947.

Because Alexandra was the first British princess to go to school, there was no precedence of any guidance for her, nor for how she could expect to be treated. Miss Dodds had suggested to Marina that it would be unfair to the other girls if Alexandra was to be granted any special favours because of her position, and Marina agreed. As far as the school was concerned, Alexandra would receive no preferential treatment.

In fact, Alexandra did not need any such special treatment, for she was more than capable of looking after herself, and was indeed more self-reliant than many of the other girls. In some respects, the rigours of the post-war years had prepared her for school: there was an enforced restriction on clothes, for instance, and only a gym-slip school uniform and a winter cloak were allowed. This actually came as a relief for Alexandra, for she had already been obliged, both for economy and through clothing rationing, to wear Princess Margaret's cast-offs, which brought her the same difficulties as any little sister.

Princess Margaret was small, and was being overtaken by the rapidly growing Alexandra, who complained to the school matron, 'She's so small, and I'm so huge!'

Alexandra was tall for her age, and very conscious of it. But she had an earnest desire to fit in with the school, an earnestness which, along with her liveliness, brought several problems. Miss Dodds recalled that Alexandra was 'very warm hearted, and demonstrative, and expressed absolutely everything she felt. She could never hide her feelings . . . and had . . . a thoroughly outgoing nature.'

Alexandra was especially careful to bear in mind all the advice about how a Princess should behave, and was suffering agonies lest she should be considered to be any different from her friends. It was not easy for Alexandra to know how to react to others, for her experience in mixing with children of her age had been rather limited. Her openness and honesty were completely disarming, and she was always protective and helpful towards the younger girls. When she herself committed some error, she would often throw her arms around whoever she had offended, and was if anything overprofuse in her apologies.

This effort was even more of an achievement than it seemed, for Alexandra was harbouring a secret that would soon undermine her claims to be like other girls in the eyes of her schoolmates. Alexandra was proud to be chosen as one of the eight bridesmaids for the wedding of Princess Elizabeth and the Duke of Edinburgh to take place at Westminster Abbey on 20 November 1947. It must have been tempting for Alexandra to tell the exciting news to the other girls at school, but she was learning the royal art of discretion, and kept it a secret until the official announcement. When the news broke, she must have undergone a noisy inquisition, not least about the dress. But as usual, great care was taken to prevent any leak of the details of the bridesmaids' costumes as well as of the bridal gown itself.

Norman Hartnell had to work under difficult circumstances, for clothing was still rationed and controlled by clothing coupons. During Alexandra's mid-term holiday, however, she was fitted out with a dress which was beyond any eleven-year-old schoolgirl's wildest dream. Partly inspired by several works of art in the Royal Collection, the bridesmaids' dresses were of spangled white tulle with fichu tops, floral headdresses, and trailing bouquets. Alexandra looked absolutely dazzling in it, and if she was nervous during the ceremony, she was consoled by her younger brother Michael, who at only five, was a train-bearer. He carefully carried the long silk and satin tulle Court train of Princess Elizabeth.

After the wedding, there were the traditional balcony appearances at Buckingham Palace, but Alexandra missed hers through thoughtfully stopping to talk to an old member of the Royal family, who sat inside the palace near the balcony. Eventually, the noise died down, and the day was over. Marina had decided that her daughter was too young to take part in the family celebrations, so Alexandra returned to Heathfield early in the evening.

When Alexandra returned there, she was of course mobbed by her excited friends, pressing her for every last detail of the event. But Alexandra refused to be drawn – she would only say how delicious the food had been at the wedding breakfast.

In fact Alexandra had felt rather embarrassed about the whole affair, and when Miss Dodds suggested that the whole school should visit Ascot the following week, when there was to be a cinema showing of the wedding, Alexandra was extremely upset, and declared that she did not want to attend. It was perhaps a strange reaction for one who had now enjoyed the full public limelight, and would be obliged to be in it all her life. At that time, however, Alexandra was as shy as any other girl her age, and could not bear the thought of being seen on film by her friends. It was not the moment to remind the young girl of the future ordeals she would have to endure, and wisely, Miss Dodds excused the delighted Alexandra from the Ascot visit, and told her she could remain in her room if she wished.

Princess Alexandra's character, then, did not escape the contradictions of her situation. She disliked being thought of as someone special, but at school she was also aware of ways in which she could use her position to advantage, although never to her own benefit. When Alexandra heard that one of her friends was in trouble, she would try to take the blame herself, realizing that if the culprit was a princess, little fuss would be made.

However her desire and inclination to be an ordinary girl was not always so laudable. Alexandra was remembered by a teacher at Heathfield as often being in trouble as the leader of a gang of 'St Trinian's type heroines'. The Heathfield staff were faced with a problem, for while they did not wish to upset Marina with reports of Alexandra's mischief, they felt strongly that she should be treated exactly like the other girls. Eventually Miss Dodds did telephone Marina, who confirmed the original policy of no preferential treatment. The outcome was that Alexandra should be kept in school for some mischief during a half-term break.

Fortunately, Alexandra was too lively to lose her sense of fun, and soon recovered from her punishment. On one occasion, the St Trinian's heroine accidentally threw a bucket of water over the matron, who had unexpectedly entered the dormitory at just the wrong moment. On another evening, she led a particularly rowdy pillow fight, causing such a noise that the long-suffering matron told the startled girls that they had nearly brought down the chandelier in the head's study on the floor below. The wrongdoers were ordered to bed at once, with instructions that the head of the dormitory was to report to Miss Dodds the following morning. The head of the dormitory was Alexandra herself, who had been chosen because she could always be relied upon to lead any high spirited romp and when she met Miss Dodds the following morning, she naturally glanced up at the chandelier. 'It's only a little chandelier,' Alexandra remarked. 'I thought it was a huge one like they have at Windsor.' She seemed relieved, but Miss Dodds smartly replied that nevertheless *she* liked it, and Alexandra, rather abashed, apologized on behalf of her dormitory for the rumpus that had been caused.

Even when Alexandra took part in the domestic duties that she shared with the other girls her lively spirits could not be suppressed. The other girls were particularly amused when, sweeping out the corridors with a large broom, and with obvious enjoyment, Alexandra called out in a good cockney accent, 'I'm the new char, Mrs Mopp, and can I do yer now?'

During school holidays, Marina took her family to seaside resorts, often to Bexhill, in Sussex. In 1949, however, when Prince Edward was at Balmoral, Marina flew with Michael and Alexandra to Jersey, but an outbreak of polio there forced the family to retreat quickly. They went instead to Clymping, in Sussex, where Marina had managed to book a hotel. Away from her school friends, Alexandra missed having companions of her own age, and Marina had made quite sure that there were to be young children staying there. The hotel staff were amused when Alexandra checked out her younger brother's room for comfort, and then gave them a letter to post, addressed simply to 'His Majesty The King, Balmoral'.

The following year, 1950, the family returned safely to Jersey, where they learned that Princess Elizabeth had given birth to her second child, Princess Anne. As soon as the Kents were back in London, Alexandra insisted on seeing the new baby, because she soon had to return to Heathfield.

By now, the Princess had settled into the routine of school life, and had conquered many of the old problems that had made Marina anxious. The term passed quickly and happily for Alexandra. She was looking forward to the school Christmas dance, for she had invited her brother Edward to be her partner, of whom she was already very proud. Unfortunately though, he was prevented from attending because of a foot operation, and once back at Coppins, caught an attack of measles, so that he had not even recovered by Christmas, and Alexandra celebrated her fourteenth birthday on Christmas Day without the company of her isolated, bed-bound brother.

Alexandra herself suffered from adenoid trouble, but after an operation during the Easter holidays, her noisy habit of snoring loudly was cured and she was well enough to prepare for the next big event, her confirmation in the summer term. Alexandra was one of the most enthusiastic of candidates. It was noticed that she would often remain longer than the other girls in the school chapel, and once even had to be tactfully dissuaded from saying her prayers out loud.

The confirmation was to be more than a personal landmark, for the school learned with great pleasure that Queen Mary would arrive with Princess Marina for the service. A red carpet was organized to be placed between the chapel and the dining-room, and to please Queen Mary the chef baked a chocolate cake made from her favourite recipe. Then the school heard, much to its general annoyance, that Queen

Mary did not wish to take tea with the parents and the girls, but would instead enjoy the company of Alexandra, Marina and the headmistress only. To make up for the disappointment, the school and parents would be allowed to wave to Queen Mary and Princess Marina as they left after tea in the royal car. But this was to be only the first disappointment.

The day before the confirmation, Queen Mary's secretary telephoned to say that Queen Mary had caught influenza, and would be unable to attend Alexandra's service. Buckingham Palace cheered everything up, though, when a message came from Queen Elizabeth that she would arrive instead of Queen Mary, and, as an added bonus, would be delighted to join the whole school for tea with the parents.

Unfortunately, it was all to no avail. Like the Christmas before, it was all to end in disappointment for Alexandra and her school. The Princess woke on the great day feeling unwell; she was told by the matron that she had caught measles. It was a bitter blow for Alexandra, for she had been looking forward to the event with great enthusiasm. The school was equally disappointed. As the confirmation service was not attended by Alexandra there were consequently no royal visitors.

The King heard of Alexandra's unhappiness sympathetically, and rather than let her wait for the next service at Heathfield, suggested that she might like to be confirmed in a royal chapel of her own choice, when she had recovered from her illness. One month later, Alexandra set off with Miss Dodds and four schoolfriends for the tiny Victorian chapel at the Royal Lodge, Windsor, which she had chosen. The King was feeling unwell, and was at first in a grumpy mood. Alexandra overheard a slight argument between her uncle and Queen Elizabeth, and remarked, 'Oh why can't they wait until I've done!'

Alexandra made her vows in a solemn voice, and with peace restored went with her friends and Miss Dodds to take tea with George VI and Queen Elizabeth at Windsor. There the King told Miss Dodds that he '. . . wanted Alexandra to have the broadest possible education, and to learn how to rub shoulders with the world and keep up with it'.

It was no doubt an aim all present would have supported, but it was perhaps not the best moment to inform Alexandra, who was becoming increasingly conscious of herself and of her appearance as she entered adolescence. She insisted on comparing herself with her elegant mother, who was always so poised, calm, and exceptionally dressed. Marina set an example which would intimidate almost any daughter especially one like Alexandra who did not obviously share her mother's natural flair for clothes.

Many considered that Marina at times lacked sympathy for her daughter and her predicament during these difficult years, but in fact Marina was very careful in her approach to Alexandra perhaps because she herself had suffered from a certain amount of strictness in her own childhood. Nevertheless Alexandra felt awkward and confused, and her initial pleasure on learning that she was to travel to France disappeared when she heard Marina had arranged for Alexandra and Edward to dine without her, as guests of the Count of Paris. The Count would later play an important role in Alexandra's education, but the Princess was so lacking in confidence that she dreaded meeting him, and was terrified that she would disgrace her mother by saying something silly or knocking something over. Miss Dodds was perhaps more skilful in helping young women to overcome their problems than Marina, and listened kindly to Alexandra's fears. She told Alexandra that she was certain she would enjoy herself, gave her hints on how to cope with conversation, and during a long talk helped to give the reassurance needed.

As had been prophesied, Alexandra had a wonderful time exploring Paris, and enjoyed her dinner with the Count. After Paris, she moved on with Edward to stay in an old converted mill in Provence and there learnt that Edward, much to his delight, was to leave Eton and change to a school in Switzerland. As Edward approached his seventeenth birthday, Alexandra was to see less of him: it had also been decided that he would be old enough to accompany Marina on a long tour of the Far East.

Back in Britain, however, the family were reunited, although only temporarily. The Kents were together at Balmoral for the summer of 1951, and their visit coincided with a holiday the King was having there. Shortly afterwards, he left for London to have an operation for the removal of a lung. What he did not know was that he was suffering from cancer, but in fact, it was feared that his life was even more in danger from a possible heart attack. The operation seemed to have been successful, but while Alexandra was at Heathfield, and Marina in Germany with Edward, the King died on 6 February 1952. He had enjoyed a shoot the day before, and went to bed early. A night watchman in the garden had been the last person to see George VI alive as the King fastened his bedroom window a little after midnight. His body was found by a valet who had brought the King his morning tea. The heart attack that everyone had feared was diagnosed as the cause of death.

# 5

# *The Coronation*

ALEXANDRA RECEIVED THE news of her uncle's death from Miss Dodds, who was understanding as ever, and helped the Princess to write letters of condolence to Queen Mary, and to Queen Elizabeth. She went with Marina and Edward to pay homage to the King, whose coffin lay on the catafalque in Westminster Hall. Later, she watched Edward, as head of the Kent family, take his place behind the gun carriage, as the late King was borne to the vault at Windsor.

It was difficult for Alexandra to realize that her cousin Princess Elizabeth, only ten years older than herself, was now Queen. Inevitably, some of the duties that had been Princess Elizabeth's would devolve on to Princess Margaret, and her share would partly pass to Alexandra, but it was wisely decided that there would be no immediate rush to train Alexandra for the burden of public duties. Nevertheless, the Princess herself was anxious to do something to help, and during a visit to Queen Mary in the Easter of 1952 Lady Airlie, her grandmother's Lady in Waiting, suggested that Alexandra should be made Patron of the Junior Red Cross. Lady Airlie was an executive member of the Red Cross, and knew enough about the organization to assure Alexandra that it would be a very suitable start.

Alexandra, glad to be of help, happily agreed, and the announcement was made official in August, just before the family made their annual visit to Balmoral. This time, their Scottish holiday included a sad journey to the spot on the lonely hillside where the Duke of Kent had been killed ten years previously. It was the first time that Alexandra had been there, and she walked with Edward and Marina across the hills to where a sombre granite cross had been placed. One way and another Alexandra's year had been one of sudden and often sombre awakening to the adult world.

It was noticed that Alexandra was nearly as tall as her mother and was acquiring a look of beauty which would soon match Marina's. She was now fifteen, and with her future still uncertain, she left Heathfield to prepare for the coronation of her cousin, to be Queen Elizabeth II. Norman Hartnell had again been chosen to design the costumes, and Alexandra was pleasantly taken aback when she saw the gown he had prepared for her, which Hartnell himself described as a 'diaphanous garment of white lace and tulle, lightly threaded with gold'. It incorporated some of the details of the gown Hartnell had designed for Alexandra to wear at Princess Elizabeth's wedding, but it was much more striking, and for a time Alexandra could not believe that she would ever match its beauty. Later, however, as the fittings progressed, she gained in confidence, and thought less of herself as the ugly duckling.

On the June morning of the Coronation, the Kents left Buckingham Palace in the second coach, at 9.40, and Alexandra was strikingly beautiful. When they reached the Abbey, Alexandra's train was carried by the Hon. Katharine Smith, and many who had scarcely seen Alexandra in public before remarked at length on her radiant appearance as she paid homage to the new Queen. Despite the awful strain of the day, Alexandra did not hurry off to bed after the celebrations. The cheering crowds who stood outside Buckingham Palace waiting for the appearance of the new Queen Elizabeth had caught Alexandra's imagination as completely as she had captivated them. Protected from the light drizzle with a raincoat, and a headscarf which also served as disguise, and accompanied by her wartime guardians, the Duke and Duchess of Beaufort, Alexandra stepped unobtrusively out of the Palace by a side door. On their way out, they met Princess Margaret and Group Captain Peter Townsend, who had the same idea – to join the cheering crowds. Unrecognized in the squash of people, Alexandra joined the chorus of seemingly unending cries of 'We want the Queen!', a novel experience for a princess. It was an exciting end to a perfect day, and one which had been a triumph for Alexandra, when she had taken her place with the other more experienced members of the royal family, and had managed to add her own beauty to the dazzling splendour of the solemn occasion.

The public gaze of the Coronation, televised as it was throughout the country, had been a forceful introduction to what Alexandra would in the future have to become used to. Moments when she could step into a crowd unnoticed would now become increasingly rare. Indeed, celebrity soon exacted its price. Not long afterwards, Alexandra was asked to present the prizes in the local secondary school near Iver, and arrived in state in her mother's car. It was a strange experience for one who had so recently been at school herself to congratulate pupils, and admire the rooms which had been specially prepared for the royal visit. Intensely nervous, Alexandra was taken to the domestic science room, where tea awaited her, and promptly dropped her cup, which broke into pieces. To everyone's horror, she picked up the bits herself. This was something which was quite natural to Alexandra, but not considered quite royal by some of her onlookers. It was a small gesture, but it hinted at a certain unstuffy aspect of Alexandra's nature. Far from suppressing it, the Princess would encourage her informal approach in the future.

Alexandra was seen as a Buckingham Palace Garden Party and her clothes came in for a great deal of criticism from some of the popular newspapers. It was an irony, they said, that Marina looked much younger than her forty-eight years, while her daughter looked twice her age of sixteen. One paper complained that 'Alexandra dressed in a blue and white dress in a beltless almost shapeless style', declaring that it was 'too long for a teenager'. Her beige shoes with cotton-reel heels and pointed toes did not escape censure either; in the opinion of the same newspaper, they resembled 'those worn by the late Queen Mary'. It was true that the outfit made Alexandra look prim and dowdy, something which could soon be rectified by the 'teens and twenty' departments of London fashion stores. Ironically, the blame for Alexandra's appearance was placed firmly on Marina, whom the critics felt had modelled her daughter on memories of herself when young. The paper was not short of advice – they pronounced that she must refuse to accept the old-maid hair style of stiff waves, should wear a fitted belt, and concluded by reminding Marina that she had as a young woman been a leader of fashion, and it was time that teenagers were talking of the Alexandra look.

It was unkind criticism, but unfortunately contained more than a measure of truth. There was little that Alexandra could do about the situation herself, for she had to be guided in her choice of clothes by her mother, but Marina had in her turn been subjected to advice from Princess Helen and was still in some ways influenced by the rigidity of the ideas of her childhood. She had been restricted in her choice of jewellery, for example, and nothing which was not 'real' could be worn, no matter how attractive a piece it might be. Marina was of course, simply passing on advice she had been given a generation previously, but for the sensitive Alexandra, it was a cause for regret that she was so out of touch with contemporary fashion.

Alexandra was glad to escape for a holiday to Greece in the summer of 1953, away from the harassment of the British press. It was the first time she had been to her mother's own country, and she was understandably excited at the prospect. Marina and Michael were also with her, and the party was met at Athens airport by King Paul of the Hellenes official representative. But they had not completely escaped public gossip. The King was Marina's cousin, and with the close family tie there was some speculation that his thirteen-year-old son, Crown Prince Constantine, might eventually become Alexandra's husband. Nothing was further from the Princess's thoughts, however, as she explored the beauties of Athens, and she enjoyed a carefree holiday. Later the Kents visited Corfu, where they were joined by other members of the royal family at a house called Mon Repos, the birthplace of Prince Philip.

While in Greece, the next stage in Alexandra's education was discussed, and it was agreed that she should attend a famous finishing school in Paris, run by a Mademoiselle Anita. Perhaps Marina had paid attention to the press comments on her daughter's appearance, for the Paris school would no doubt offer impeccable advice on matters of dress as well as teaching more formal subjects. When the Kents returned to London, the formal announcement was made that Alexandra would attend the school, and that while in Paris she would be the guest of Henri d'Orleans, Count of Paris, and his family.

Once again this put Alexandra's name in the news, for the Count was the Pretender to the French throne. Apart from being descended from the brother of Louis XIV, he was also the grandson of Louis Philippe, who had briefly restored the French throne in 1830. As a Bourbon in the French Republic, the Count of Paris had been prevented from living in France by an act of 1886, and the act had only been revoked as recently as 1950, when the danger was considered to be over. The Count had returned to his country and taken a house near Versailles, on the strict understanding that he and his family would take no part in public affairs.

In fact, his presence alone was more influential than the government could have imagined. The Count's arrival in France apparently increased the number of royalist supporters there to more than five million, a figure which worried the ardent republicans. Fears were expressed that with Alexandra's connection with the Count and his family, and her own place in the British royal family, newly revived monarchist feeling might lead to the Count being restored to the French throne. A French Government spokesman made a cautionary statement that 'although France adores the British royal family, they could not understand why the Count of Paris had been chosen as Princess Alexandra's host'.

In fact, there was no ulterior motive. Marina was related to the Count's sister, and this, coupled with the knowledge that one of the Count's daughters was also to be a pupil at the finishing school, had made his home an obvious choice. The rumours were quite unfounded, for it was revealed that the Count of Paris was a strong socialist, and he even published his political views in a monthly news-letter.

Before leaving for France, Alexandra accompanied her mother on a tour of Lancashire, but all did not go well, as the visit, covering over 200 miles and lasting three days, was unfortunately badly organized by the Cotton Board. The schedule of the various events was impossible to maintain, and the programme had to be constantly altered and adapted; in the three days the Kents were expected to visit five cotton mills, a college, an exhibition, a research centre, three town halls and to shake hands with over four hundred people. Marina and Alexandra, through no fault of their own, were late for every function except the first. In an effort to try and keep to the schedule, the royal car had been forced to drive at breakneck speeds, but to no avail. It was not surprising that at the final mayoral tea party on the last day, Alexandra looked pale and strained.

Neither was the tour a boost to her public image. There were far too many officials to be presented, something which upset those who had bought new clothes for the visit and had to be left out. Because of the bad planning, Marina and Alexandra had no time to look at anything which was of special interest, and almost nobody was able to catch sight of the Royal visitors.

The Lancashire tour was an unpleasant introduction to Alexandra of a sample of the kind of duties she would have so often in the future to undertake, although hopefully events would not always be so badly organized. But despite the discomfort Alexandra felt from the start, she displayed the kind of thoughtfulness which would become the hallmark of her public personality. Several times she insisted that the chauffeur slow down so that the crowds who had been waiting in the rain would not be disappointed. The visit too, had a character which Alexandra would, in the future, always protest against: the prominence of the official rather than the ordinary person whom she preferred to meet.

It had been a gruelling and dispiriting trip, but, as Alexandra was fast discovering, there is little rest for a twentieth-century princess. She had little time to recover from her ordeal in London, and left almost at once for Paris in mid-October 1953.

# 6

# *Paris Days*

BEFORE JOINING THE Count and his family in Versailles, and facing the rigours of Mademoiselle Anita's school, Alexandra and Marina spent a week with Alexandra's Aunt, Princess Olga of Yugoslavia and her cousin Princess Elizabeth, in their small Paris flat. Alexandra was shown Paris by Princess Elizabeth, and spent a relaxing week enjoying the shops and cafés. After entertaining the Count for dinner and discussing the arrangements for her daughter's home, Marina flew back to London, and Alexandra was driven by Princess Olga to Louveciennes, near Versailles, site of the Count's home, the *Manoir du Coeur Volant* (Manor of the Flying Heart).

It was an old fifteen-bedroomed manor that Alexandra was brought to, but even that was too small for the Count and his wife, for they had eleven children. The youngest two, Claude and Thibault, spoke no English, and it was decided that to help Alexandra's French, they would be the ones to share with her the little whitewashed cottage near the house, called *Blanche Neige* (Snow White).

The family was a large but happy one and was used to creating its own amusements as television was forbidden. After the company of so many girls at Heathfield, Alexandra quickly adapted to her new surroundings and her new companions. She became particularly friendly with Henri, the Dauphin, then at university, and also his elder sister Princess Isabelle, who was twenty-one, and studying for her final nursing exams. Princess Anne, at fifteen was to start at the finishing school with Alexandra, and on the first day, and for the rest of the term, the Count drove his daughter and Alexandra to the Rue de l'Amiral d'Estaing on his way to his office.

The exterior of the building at No. 10 was almost as forbidding as its owner, Mademoiselle Anita. In retrospect, Heathfield seemed like a holiday. There was no opportunity for high jinks here, for Mademoiselle believed in a 'no nonsense' approach to education. Each girl was issued with a list of rules that could not fail to daunt any newcomer, and when Mademoiselle Anita was asked by British newspapers about Alexandra, she replied stiffly, 'Which Princess? I have five in my school.'

Many of the girls came from conventional schools, bringing to Paris boisterous behaviour more suited to the hockey field than the drawing-room. It did not take long for the girls to learn that Mademoiselle's girls must 'move with elegance, must not clatter up and down stairs or tap their heels as they walk. They must never shout or raise their voices, laugh or giggle loudly.' As for dress, a subject important to Alexandra, any inclination to overdress was quickly suppressed. 'Good taste' was the chief aim of the school; accordingly, 'No elegant young woman ever looks painted. Ladies *never* wear large ear-rings.'

The school aimed to give in Mademoiselle's words, 'lessons in living'. Apart from deportment, Princess Alexandra learnt typewriting, shorthand, housekeeping skills, and even laundering. As if that was not enough, there was a special course in languages, for Mademoiselle believed that 'English, French and Spanish were essential to any girl in society'. To back up this awesome programme, Alexandra would then have classes in Russian literature, delivered in French. Needless to say, their lessons were all given by women, as male teachers could only be an unnecessary distraction to the girls. It must have been with considerable relief that Alexandra escaped with her friends on their weekly free afternoon to tour art galleries and, more importantly for her, to take piano lessons with the famous teacher Mlle Labroquère, who had been a pupil of Cortot. Looking back, there must be doubts about how much the finishing school contributed to Alexandra's development. Certainly in some respects, it did not prepare its pupils for reality in its wider worldly aspects – if Alexandra had only learned how to behave in drawing-room society, it would have been unlikely she would have had the distinctive personality and understanding of problems outside her own sphere which have come to make her so many friends.

Alexandra was undoubtedly given an unofficial training, though, through her contact with the Count and his socialist views. The Princess was not converted to any political dogma, but was impressed by witnessing the example of the Count's daughter, Princess Isabelle. The French princess had worked for part of her nursing training in the slum districts of Paris, spending much time helping motherless families to create a balanced diet, and she would still often return there to nurse the sick in the filthiest conditions. Often she would return home and regale her family and Alexandra with gruesome tales of her experiences. Her family were quick to give her the nickname 'Frankenstein', because of the stories she recounted. While such experiences might be shrugged off as unimportant by some, the horror of poverty and poor social conditions made an unforgettable impression on Alexandra. She had, of course, heard of Marina's early struggles in Paris, but in the Count's household she came into almost direct contact with aspects of life far removed from her own. They were to remain with her, and give her a concern for the underprivileged, for the rest of her life, and undoubtedly influenced her more than the finishing school.

Alexandra returned to England to spend her seventeenth birthday on Christmas Day with her family at Iver. It was a happy occasion, for Edward had passed his military exams at Sandhurst, Michael was home from his preparatory school, and Marina was also host to their Yugoslavian cousins. More notably, they were joined by the Stoeckls, who lived in a cottage in the grounds of Coppins, and also a family called Koziells, Polish refugees who had arrived in England almost destitute and whom Marina, in a typically kind gesture, had helped financially, by arranging for them to stay rent free in a small house at Coppins.

After Christmas, Alexandra herself returned to Paris for her final term with Mademoiselle Anita. During her brief visit to England, her family were sure that she had benefited from her education at the finishing school. Most obvious was the abrupt change in her appearance, for gone were the tweedy clothes, and in their place were the new Paris fashion. A new hair style only emphasized her elegance, and when Alexandra completed her final three months in Paris and finally returned to England, the fashion writers were delighted with her appearance.

Not long after Alexandra was back in Coppins, the Kents were joined by Princess Olga of Yugoslavia and her son Prince Nicholas, but their pleasant company was soon marred by another unexpected tragedy. The young Prince set off for London after playing a game of tennis with friends at Winkfield, and as he approached Dachet his car skidded and overturned into a flooded ditch. Help arrived, but too late – Prince Nicholas had been killed outright. It was a terrible shock for Marina, and to her fell the additional pain of breaking the sad news to her sister

Olga. It was only twelve years since she had received the report of her husband's death, and the death of her young nephew revived the horror of that night. Alexandra too had been devoted to her cousin, but nobly decided to carry out the long awaited engagement that had been planned by the Junior Red Cross despite her sense of grief.

This was symptomatic of the new life Alexandra was leading. As soon as she returned from Paris, great changes and plans for her future were being organized. The Princess was due to start her public duties in earnest now that Mademoiselle Anita's finishing school had completed the preparations. There never had been any doubt that Alexandra would take a share of the burden of royal duties, of course, but the particular circumstances that year meant that her talents were all the more in demand. The younger members of the royal family numbered only Princess Margaret, the Queen and Prince Philip, and as the Queen planned to visit a large part of the Commonwealth, someone was needed to help out at home.

At the time, there was some wide-ranging speculation about Alexandra's future. Her rather unconventional schooling, unprecedented for a British princess, had led some commentators to suppose that she would perhaps be allowed to assume an equally novel public role and take a job somewhere. Indeed, many modern thinkers considered that a young person's life to be ordered around a string of tedious functions was completely unfair. Many of Alexandra's friends had taken 'ordinary' jobs; Princess Margaritha of Baden-Baden had become a probationer nurse at St Thomas's Hospital, London; Camilla Straight, daughter of the Chairman of BOAC, had gone to New York to work in a department store; and Princess Isabelle d'Orleans still worked in the Paris hospital where she had trained.

But the demands of Alexandra's special position would not be ignored. Although the princess was 'only' the Queen's cousin, and was unlikely ever to succeed, at the time she began her public life she was closer in line to the crown. Moreover, Alexandra was far better qualified than some members of the royal family to cope with public duties by dint of this very same unusual education, for she had moved in a wider social context than anyone else in her family, and had gained valuable experience and understanding by doing so.

Nevertheless, it was not a decision to be taken lightly. Since Alexandra had already enjoyed a glimpse of ordinary life, she must have felt rather daunted at the prospect of a life which could never be quite her own. But whatever her own feelings were, Alexandra was too valuable an asset to waste as a royal ambassador. It was the understanding of areas of society into which she had not been expected to move, combined with an inherited sense of dignity, that would make Alexandra a success. She was never ill at ease with classes other than her own, and there would be none of the remoteness sometimes attached to the image of the Queen and Princess Margaret.

To help her in the new public role, Marina had already appointed Lady Moyra Hamilton as Lady-in-Waiting to her daughter. The wide-ranging duties of this most inconspicuous of royal attendants are fairly onerous, and must have constituted a daunting prospect. Lady Moyra would have to be both unobtrusive and readily available, would have to be ready to hand a speech to her mistress, or take a bouquet, even to provide a needle and thread if that was what was needed.

The choice of Lady Moyra was a wise one. It was important that Lady Moyra should guide her mistress where necessary, but at the same time, allow Alexandra the chance to develop her own personality without swamping her. She was several years older than Alexandra, and already a friend. Her background was, of course, impeccable, being the daughter of the Duke of Abercorn from County Tyrone, Northern Ireland, and also sharing many of Alexandra's interests such as riding and music. Moreover, Lady Moyra had a sense of humour, something vitally important for anyone working with Alexandra and was also, fortunately, several inches taller than Alexandra, who was often conscious of her own height.

Life was changing very rapidly for the Princess who once said that given her way, she would like to 'grow up like Mother, marry a farmer, give lots of cosy parties, hunt for five days a week, and come to London only once a week'.

# 7

# Canadian Adventure

THE PUBLIC WERE quick to notice the change in Alexandra's appearance. In May 1954 she went with Marina to the British Industries Fair, the first time Alexandra had been seen in public since her return from Paris. This time, as she inspected the stalls at the Fair, no one accused her of wearing Queen Mary's clothes. In her simple dark linen button-through frock, she was considered to be the most elegant woman there. The old maidish hairstyle had gone, and Alexandra was dubbed 'the New Princess'. When questioned about her pupil's transformation, though, Mademoiselle Anita refused to take any credit. 'I have not changed your princess,' she commented; 'it is Paris that has done that.'

The reports of the 'new look' princess must have pleased Alexandra, and helped to give her confidence any help it needed. Now she could tackle large events on her own. Nearly two years since it was discussed with Queen Mary and Lady Airlie, the Junior Red Cross met in a room at St James's Palace, where Alexandra was appointed their Patron. The reception for over 150 guests was something of an ordeal for her, surrounded as she was by the severe portraits of her ancestors. After the Chairman pinned a Patron's badge of gold, diamonds and rubies onto Alexandra's dark blue Red Cross uniform, the Princess made her first public speech. In an unexpectedly low voice, Alexandra told them that she was

. . . very proud to have this opportunity of meeting so many of you. I want to thank you for this badge, which as Patron I shall always be very glad to wear and keep, in token of my association with the Junior Red Cross. Thank you for your kind welcome. I wish you every success in your work.

Competent if uninspiring, perhaps, but after reading the speech, which took about thirty seconds in all, Alexandra completely disarmed everyone present by saying in a loud voice, 'Was I awful?'

It was a typical flash of her own openness, and not a disaster; Alexandra was of course being 'tried out' in fairly relaxing circumstances, for the guests were nearly all young children who were not particularly critical. But the event gave an indication of what would become only too familiar – 145 hands had to be shaken, and no matter how nervous Alexandra felt and would feel, she would always be expected to produce a charming smile.

The Red Cross function was a beginning, even if Alexandra did lose her handbag once and her gloves twice during the afternoon tea of sandwiches and eclairs. There was, however, no doubting the delightful charm which broke through her nerves. When some small boy who was presented to Alexandra forgot to address her as 'Ma'am' and said instead, 'Wotcher!' he received a cheerful 'Wotcher!' in reply from the Princess herself. Alexandra had made an instant success of her first important solo engagement, and officials there only regretted that the late Queen Mary could not have seen her grand-daughter.

Despite the acclaim Alexandra was given her audience, the press were uncertain about how to accept Alexandra. Her style was, after all, surprisingly informal, and they were not sure how to interpret what they considered as 'over familiar' behaviour which was, in their opinion, anything but royal. Perhaps more to the point was their disappointment that they could not hear what the Princess had said.

Over the next few months, at a variety of contrasting functions, Alexandra quickly picked up the experience needed to project herself graciously to the public. She no longer made remarks, which the press could eagerly pick up, such as a previous lapse when she asked 'Do I have to carry this about?' when presented with a bouquet. She toured the depots of the Alexandra Rose Day, named after her great-grandmother, wife of Edward VII, and on the evening of 2 June 1956, attended her first public ball, the Rose Ball, at Grosvenor House, where Alexandra looked absolutely radiant in her Hartnell-designed gown, appropriately embroidered with a rose motif. She accepted new patronages, such as the Royal Alexandra Hospital for Sick Children, and travelled to Scotland to launch her first ship. While Alexandra was there, she was concerned to hear that the young Duke of Kent had been involved in a motor accident and was knocked unconscious, but fears that he might have suffered brain damage were proved unfounded when Edward was admitted to the National Hospital for Nervous Diseases. The news that her brother was unharmed, cheered up

Alexandra, and she swung the bottle at the *British Soldier* with a heartfelt smile.

The engagements quickly piled in, and Alexandra was glad to return to relax in the peace of her home in Iver when she was able. She would often help Marina with gardening, or play a game of croquet on the well-kept lawn. In the evening, Marina would often receive dinner guests from the world of art, and familiar figures who dined with the Kents included Noël Coward, Laurence Olivier, and Sir Malcolm Sargent. The famous conductor was a particular favourite at Coppins, and had often bathed Alexandra when she was a small baby. Thanks to Mademoiselle Anita, Alexandra was no longer tongue-tied in such company, and was able to demonstrate her accomplishment as a pianist, often playing for guests before dinner.

Although Coppins had been an attractive house, there were certain disadvantages, which became more obvious now that Alexandra was involved in public life, chiefly its inconvenient distance from London, and Marina was pleased when the Queen offered her the rooms in Kensington Palace which had been vacant since the death of Princess Louise in 1939. Queen Elizabeth had first offered the apartment to Marina after the Duke of Kent's death, but bombs had partly destroyed the roof and hasty war-time repairs had subsequently encouraged dry rot. Renovation work was to be carried out while Marina and Alexandra were in Canada in August, and hopefully the rooms would be ready when they returned.

A visit to Canada had been arranged by the Government, for Marina and Alexandra, to help promote trade figures. It was the first major tour for Marina since the war, and especially exciting for Alexandra who had not been abroad often.

Much had to be done in preparation for the visit not least the assembling of Alexandra's wardrobe. A favourite designer of Marina's, John Cavanagh, showed Alexandra the drawings he had made for various simple clothes. Cavanagh was astonished at the many imaginative suggestions that the young Princess contributed herself, although in some respects she was still ruled by the conservative outlook of Mademoiselle Anita. But Alexandra overcame her scruples and reluctantly agreed to allow a frock with buttons, forbidden by the Paris finishing school, on the grounds that it was meant to be functional and not ornamental.

Early in August, with Cavanagh's creations carefully packed, Alexandra and Marina flew to Canada in a V.I.P. plane provided by the Royal Canadian Air Force. Lady Moyra Hamilton was there to wait on Alexandra, and Marina took her long-serving Lady-in-Waiting, Lady Rachel Davidson.

The Canadians knew very little about Alexandra, and were uncertain whether to give her visit the prominence due to a royal newcomer, or to play the visit down. By chance, a variety of hampering rules seemed to make inevitable the latter treatment. The rules were strict indeed. No press or amateur photographers were to use their cameras within 15 ft of Marina or Alexandra, and neither would the authorities allow any 'surprise' pictures. No one would be allowed to talk to the royal couple without prior arrangement, and there would be no press conference.

These stiff protocol rules had been arranged in consultation with Marina's office from the best of motives, chiefly to protect Alexandra. It is quite unlikely from her own lively character that she agreed with all the strictures, for they went against her own views of openness and courtesy, and in future when she was able and when she was more confident of her ability to handle crowds, Alexandra would waive aside such formalities. For the time being, however, the Princess had to do as she was advised.

Many Canadians themselves were displeased by the restrictions. The *Toronto Telegram*, especially annoyed, wrote that 'royalty suffer from the officiousness of underlings who fail to realize that their excessive precautions are an embarrassment to those they serve, and an insult to the public'. It finished crossly, 'The security arrangements for the tour are obnoxious and absurd.'

This Canadian popular reaction against the treatment of their visitors as untouchables partly arose from the more relaxed social atmosphere in their country. Ordinary Canadians found it difficult to accept that British royalty could possibly be expected to behave in a stuffy manner. What they had seen of the young and cheerful Alexandra, and the elegant Marina, only made the press more resolute to break down the barriers that had been imposed against them. Several photographers refused to accept the rules, and when the Kents arrived at Quebec airport, to be met by the Governor-General, Vincent Massey, they pushed forward and took shots of the visitors 6 ft nearer than was allowed. No one objected.

45

Marina and Alexandra stayed in Government House in Quebec, and one night soon after their arrival Alexandra slipped out with Lady Moyra after dinner and took a secret ride round the old city. They were driven in a two-wheeled carriage drawn by a horse called Ginger, and their eighty-one-year-old driver also acted as guide. Alexandra was full of questions and in good humour. Neither had she lost any of her early fondness for horses and the whole ride was a joy for her; at the end of it she gratefully rewarded the driver with a large tip.

It was a welcome and rare moment of relaxation, for the Kents had to undertake a busy programme. The first journey they had to make was from Quebec to Montreal, where Marina unveiled a war memorial. To the embarrassment of officials responsible for the organization, the wreath which Marina was to lay could not be found at the last minute. It was Alexandra who saved the day, before panic set in, by taking from Lady Moyra a bouquet which had been presented to Marina, and handing it quietly to her mother.

The earlier reservations about Alexandra and Marina's Canadian tour, were quickly dispelled by the charm and friendliness of the royal couple, and equally quickly forgotten by the press, who vied with each other to snatch the best photographs of the princesses. The cameramen actually jostled with each other at Niagara Falls, where Marina had arrived to open the second largest power generating station in the world, and as Alexandra explored the turbine rooms, she was faithfully followed by a photographer. Quite unexpectedly, Alexandra grabbed a camera from her Army escort, and snapped back at the small crowd of reporters. It was a moment of inspiration and, as a bonus, the resulting photographs were good enough to be published in a Detroit newspaper with the caption, 'The Princess packs a bigger punch than Niagara!'

The tour continued successfully with a visit to Halifax, Nova Scotia, and then when it was all over, Alexandra and Lady Moyra joined the Duchess of Kent in New York. There they spent a relaxing time with friends before taking the *Queen Mary* for a leisurely sail home. Alexandra had not been overburdened with functions in Canada, but she had scored a great success, and had also learnt a great deal from watching Marina, enabling her to begin formulating her own ideas as to how foreign tours should be conducted. Although she was relatively inconspicuous, everyone who saw the young Princess had liked her, so much so that a hair style named 'Princess Sandra', copied from

Alexandra's own coiffeur, was taken up by many young girls, and was popular long after the Princess had left Canadian shores.

Canada had been exciting, but now there was the prospect of the move from Buckinghamshire to London to take Alexandra's mind off the sense of anti-climax. On their return, the palace wing was not ready, the south-west section still had to be dried out, and Marina felt that it was far too large for her family. Eventually it was decided that the wing should be divided, and one part would later be given to Princess Margaret after her marriage to Anthony Armstrong-Jones. A constant heating problem was solved by adapting a large boiler that also warmed the London Museum, then housed in Kensington Palace.

It must have been hard to keep one's mind on these domestic problems in such an historic home. The original building had been improved by Sir Christopher Wren, and the grounds extended when George II quietly annexed part of Hyde Park for his own use. In her time, Queen Mary had restored the nursery, which had been used by Queen Victoria who, the daughter of an earlier Duke of Kent, had been born there.

Perhaps Marina had little fondness for romantic legends connected with Queen Victoria, for she had the nursery suite altered to please her meticulous taste. Several Adam fireplaces, quite appropriate to the period of the rooms they were to be placed in, were brought in by the Ministry of Works, but a carping Parliament considered them an unnecessary luxury, and Marina had to pay for one of them out of her own purse.

At long last the Palace was completed, and the Kents left Coppins for their new London home. It was the perfect base, and the move up to the capital did not deprive them of the peace of their country house. They were never troubled by gazing tourists. Marina set her famous artistic flair to work, and soon made their house a beautiful home. Some of her preference for the white and gold décor which had enriched Coppins was repeated in the public rooms of Kensington Palace. The private sitting-room, in contrast with the formality of the other rooms, was welcoming to guests, as it soon took on the atmosphere of Marina and Alexandra's interests. Books, records, music, and above all, the paintings that Marina had executed herself, all helped to create a family home.

# 8

# *Nurse Alexandra*

THE EXPERIENCE THAT Alexandra had gained abroad was invaluable to her, not only for the practice it gave her in becoming skilful at her specially demanding duties, but also to let Alexandra realize how genuinely she was liked for simply being herself. Critics sometimes expected royalty still to conduct themselves like Queen Victoria, but if they looked for this in Princess Alexandra they were to be disappointed. Alexandra was demonstrating how it was possible to be royal and human at the same time. She herself is reported as saying, 'It seems to me that I am first of all a human being, and secondly a member of the royal family.'

This was, of course, a reflection of changing values throughout society. In the twentieth century royalty was never to be taken for granted, as in the past. The need for a change in the image of the monarchy was forcibly expressed by the then Lord Altrincham, a young peer who was later to renounce his title and become plain Mr John Grigg. He galvanized the debate and scandalized the establishment by penning an article in 1957 attacking the monarchy.

The Queen's entourage are almost without exception the tweedy sort . . . Buckingham Palace hierarchy has lamentably failed to live with the times . . . [while] the monarchy has become 'popular' and 'multi-racial', the court has remained a tight little enclave of English ladies and gentlemen.

The article was read by Alexandra, a sympathetic 'enemy' who was said privately to agree with much of what Altrincham had written. She herself disliked the often pompous phrases written for her to read, and would often write her speeches herself which she felt she could deliver more honestly. But Alexandra was in a difficult position, for she had more than one critical view to contend with. While she sometimes inadvertently contributed to informality in her engagements with the occasional accident, she could do nothing to refute the exaggerated accounts of them, which the press were often anxious to pin down as 'unroyal' behaviour, and she was likely to offend as many people as she encouraged. One paper reported, with more imagination than fact, that 'once Alexandra upset a table of cups in Wales, and half an hour later, one of her shoes stuck in the mud, which she had to retrieve in front of a large crowd'.

On the whole, though, Alexandra's mishaps endeared her to the press, for they were only part of her charm and genuine kindness to those she met, which could always provide a good photograph and a newsworthy story. Her brother Edward was less fortunate. He had inherited his father's impulsive nature, and had never lost the interest in cars which began when he was a small boy. Soon a series of minor crashes had fixed him in the public eye as a careless driver, and then reports spread that this had angered the Queen so much that she had banned him from driving. These stories were, of course, quite untrue and Edward was obliged to give a small press conference to clear his name. Nevertheless once the media got hold of an image of the young Duke, they would not let it go, and were ready to misinterpret any event. Perhaps more annoying than the driving exploits was a report that Edward had helped throw fully dressed guests into the Thames during a Chelsea river party. While it is true that Edward sometimes enjoyed pranks and was involved in the kind of escapade inevitable for any boy of his age, there was no doubt that the press gave him a rougher ride than he deserved. Kensington Palace issued a denial, but worse was to follow at a party for his twenty-first birthday on 9 October 1956.

The Queen, the Duke of Edinburgh, Queen Elizabeth the Queen Mother, and several other members of the royal family had attended a private family dinner given at Coppins by Marina, and afterwards two hundred guests arrived to celebrate, including a woman who claimed to have forgotten her invitation card. She managed to slip into the house, but suspicions had been aroused, and after an interview by a lady-in-waiting, the uninvited guest transpired to be a reporter, and had to be escorted out by the police. As if this were not enough, it was later discovered that two other 'guests' were also reporters. Not surprisingly, the Queen and Marina were both furious.

The result of their annoyance was a complaint to the Press Council. It read,

The Queen and the Duchess of Kent were seriously disturbed by these incidents, and Her Majesty considers that it is not too much to ask that she and other members of the royal family should receive the same privacy in their homes as is enjoyed by others. On the occasion in question their privacy was not only invaded in an improper manner, but the methods by which this was achieved bordered on deceit.

The guilt over the incident which had marred the Duke's coming-of-age celebrations helped to tone down reports on his activities, and also had the side-effect of making the press more concerned to report Alexandra's public engagements fully and accurately.

But the problems were not over. This new scrutiny led to tasteless speculation on the Kents' finances, and especially how Alexandra chose her clothes.

This drew on a long-established veil of gossip. The Kents had sometimes been referred to as the Cinderellas of the royal family, something which perhaps began because in some respects, Marina, as a foreigner had never been totally accepted by all members of the royal family. To make her introduction more difficult, she had always been desperately shy, and found all her public engagements an ordeal, although with her skill in carrying them out, this could never have been guessed. She never quite grew accustomed to certain aspects of Court life, and tended to keep in the background, which while it made her feel more comfortable, prevented her from gaining the advantages someone in her position could expect. Indeed, as a widow, she had little money, and unusual though it seems in retrospect, she was obliged to sell family objets d'art to boost her own capital. Various efforts to prove that both Princess Alexandra and Marina inherited from Queen Mary remained only speculation as the contents of royal wills are never made public.

Whatever the circumstances, Marina's years in Paris had taught her a sense of economy which she had passed to her daughter, nowhere more apparent than in her dress. Of course, Alexandra's wardrobe included a beautiful series of gowns designed for her by John Cavanagh and Norman Hartnell, but they were reserved for official occasions. For more practical everyday wear, Alexandra had many 'off-the-peg' bargains. She was often seen in department stores in Kensington selecting tasteful but inexpensive clothes, and tongues began to wag. Friends contributed to the speculation, perhaps inadvertently, by remarking how pleased the princess was when she ordered a 35s. (£1.75) duffle-coat by mail order. Not that she did not appreciate *haute couture*. She also had some clothes designed for her by Maureen Baker, of Susan Small, who later made Princess Anne's wedding dress.

Alexandra's simplistic taste in what she wore was part of her relaxed image, for she refused to be typecast into wearing one particular fashion. Queen Mary had never altered her image over the years, and was in appearance forever Edwardian. But Alexandra was more adventurous, and whatever she wore, whether a Marks and Spencer's knitted coat or a Hartnell gown, she always managed to look elegant. Her tall frame set off the slender garments she favoured, which accentuated her high cheek bones, and her sparkling blue green eyes. At the end of the day, her appearance justified her choice of dress, and silenced any gossip.

At home, Alexandra's greatest pleasure was still music, and she continued her piano lessons after leaving her Paris finishing school. For a time she had been nearly discouraged by Edward, who used to poke fun at her efforts, but she was, and still is, an extremely fine performer. Her special loves were Schubert and Chopin, but, as with her dress, she was nothing if not open-minded, and was also a keen jazz fan, and included Sinatra and other popular singers of the mid 1950s alongside classical records in her collection.

An incident soon after revealed just how deep was her love of music. When the princess was to open a Y.M.C.A. hostel in Grimsby, the organizers considered that the usual gift of a gold key was inappropriate for a girl of twenty, and they asked Alexandra what she would like to choose instead. They were surprised to learn that instead of the handbag or similar item they had expected, she had selected the harpsichord works of Scarlatti, which she could play on her piano. The complete set of his keyboard works arrived from Italy, and were bound in leather, with the added adornment of Alexandra's own personal monogram in gold. It was a pleasing touch, for the intertwining 'A's, which had been first used by her grand-mother Queen Alexandra on her personal writing paper, had only recently been adopted by Alexandra, on her eighteenth birthday. Of course the double 'A's later took on a new significance when she married Angus Ogilvy.

Another gift at the same time, an engraved glass received from an arts an crafts committee, was a similar gesture that reflected the sense of gratitude that organizations felt in having Alexandra present, with her easy conversational style. However, even this presented problems, as it sometimes encouraged over-familiarity with those who met her.

51

Consequently, Alexandra had to select her friends very carefully, and had to watch for those who felt that her natural kindness provided easy admittance into her private life. Alexandra had realized early on that for her own happiness she had to separate her public from her private life completely. But even in the early days this was not always possible, and unimportant events could become tiring performances.

At one time, shortly before she was twenty-one, Alexandra was travelling with her lady-in-waiting in a bus from Kensington to Leicester Square. She was in fact making a visit to Coutts' bank in the Strand, and might have gone unnoticed behind her headscarf had she not been spotted by a sharp-eyed photographer as they left the bus. Before they knew it, the picture was all set up, they looking rather sheepish while the proud conductress posed like a mannequin on the stairs of the bus. The Princess and Lady Moyra then walked the short distance to Coutts, where an official let them in as the bank had already closed, but when the two ladies tried to leave the building some time later they were obliged to retreat. Word had spread, and a large crowd waited outside on the Strand. Instead, someone was forced to call a taxi, and the bemused Princess departed for Kensington with Lady Moyra from a crowded doorway.

Still, Alexandra was undeterred. She would not become out of touch if she could help it, and still succeeded in sometimes passing unrecognized. During the same year, Alexandra visited the B.B.C. and there she bumped into the comedian Bob Monkhouse, who completely failed to recognize her. Assuming that Alexandra was a devoted fan, Monkhouse asked if she was interested in television, and offered her free tickets for his show. Someone overheard this, and tried to tell Monkhouse that he was talking to Princess Alexandra, but he replied slightly crossly, 'I'm the one who makes jokes around here.'

Although Alexandra was becoming popular, she herself often felt dissatisfied with her position, and the earlier doubts about the nature of her role as a public figure were surfacing again. For her, it was not enough to be regarded as a useful member of the royal family, and now she argued that she was sufficiently removed from the throne to take up a career. Naturally, this had not simply come out of the blue – Alexandra had it in her mind to enrol as a student nurse. It was something she had always been interested in, and something of a family vocation; Marina had been an auxiliary during the war, and Alexandra had been impressed by the work of Princess Isabelle, the Count of Paris's daughter.

Her naturally sympathetic and thoughtful character made her an ideal candidate, but the peculiarities of the special station in life were not so easily overcome. It is unlikely that Marina really believed that Alexandra, in her position, could ever devote her life to anything but the affairs and functions associated with the royal family, but Alexandra was insistent that she wanted to try nursing. Eventually her resolve won the day, and it was decided that she would enrol for a course in child welfare in the Great Ormond Street hospital for Sick Children, in London.

Eyebrows were raised in certain quarters at Alexandra's decision, but the Princess was convinced it could only do her good. She would, as at Heathfield, share the same conditions as her peers at the hospital, except of course that she would still have some royal duties to fulfil. If Alexandra did not care for the work, she would, like anyone else, be able to give it up.

For a member of the royal family to take up an everyday job of work was another 'first' for Alexandra. If for no other reason, it would have been worthwhile simply as a precedent. Her employment helped others in her family to take similar decisions; it certainly made it easier for Prince Richard of Gloucester to follow his architectural career.

Alexandra arrived at the Great Ormond Street Hospital one month late for enrolment, as the arrangements had been made rather hurriedly, and was slightly nonplussed to be welcomed on the first day by a bouquet from her new Matron. It was exactly what Alexandra did not want, determined as she was to be no different from the other nurses who were training there, so she set about her work with all the more vigour and openness. The other nurses were surprised to discover that Alexandra worked at all the exhausting duties with exactly the same sense of responsibility as they did, and they soon grew fond of her and her lively sense of humour. It was tiring work, even more so for the Princess than for the others, as she would often work thirteen hours a day, and then, with little sleep, put on her public face and rush off to attend some formal engagement. On one occasion at least, the appointment was actually at another hospital, where she had to inspect the wards, not with the new professional eye of a nurse, but with the gracious concern of a princess.

On Christmas Day 1957, Alexandra reached her twenty-first birthday. So that this would be more of an event and not be swallowed up by seasonal activities, the celebrations were moved from the 25th to Twelfth Night, 6 January. Marina gave a dinner for her daughter at Kensington Palace, which was attended by the Queen, Prince Philip and Queen Elizabeth the Queen Mother. Only Princess Margaret was absent, much to her regret, because of a heavy chill. The emphasis was on informality, and the two hundred guests who had been invited to a private party after the meal, were to be expected to join in some dancing. Alexandra had invited the clarinettist Sid Phillips and his band to play Dixieland Jazz.

It was a memorable evening for Alexandra, and one which those present did not forget. The beautiful Princess symbolized all that was hopeful and youthful in what had now become a prospering country. An official birthday portrait was taken by Anthony Armstrong-Jones, and in one paper appeared with the caption, 'This splendid girl is so stately and statuesque. Through her father she inherits the blue-eyed fairness, and the wonderful Windsor complexion; through her Greek mother, the chiselled features and through her brooding look of dignity, one senses a strong reliant personality.'

Quite unfairly, though, some of the press reports reflected their writers' long-standing ambivalence of attitude to Alexandra.

'Alexandra is endearingly amateurish. Before making a speech, she clears her throat and gulps nervously. She speaks so quietly that even from a few feet away, she is often inaudible. Princess Margaret has a clear, well-pronounced voice, and is wholly self-possessed.'

But happily Alexandra had by this time put herself out of reach of these ancient grudges, and they were increasingly rare. What criticism there was could be discounted, for Alexandra was in constant demand by various charities and organizations. She had become Patron of the Guide Dogs for the Blind Association, and there, as everywhere, had impressed those present by her thoughtfulness; on one occasion, she insisted on being blindfolded so that she could experience properly what it is like to be led by a dog.

This natural warmth and consideration was the reason for her popularity. A birthday party given for her by the residents of an old people's home at Iver was made memorable by the easy and genuine manner in which she spoke to her hosts. There was no sense of awkward embarrassment, and straight away she made the old people feel they

H.R.H. Prince George, Duke of Kent, in the uniform of group captain, and Princess Marina, the Duchess of Kent, with their children Prince Edward and Princess Alexandra. Photographed in the grounds of Coppins in Iver, Buckinghamshire, by Cecil Beaton in 1941 (Camera Press).

The marriage of H.R.H. Princess Alexandra to the Hon. Angus Ogilvy. The glass coach is taking them from Westminster Abbey down the Mall to St James's Palace (Camera Press).

(*opposite*) Princess Alexandra celebrated her twenty-first birthday on 25th December 1957. This birthday portrait was taken at Kensington Palace, London, by Anthony Armstrong Jones (Camera Press).

Princess Alexandra wearing the uniform of the British Red Cross of which she is Vice President. On her lapel is the Coronation Medal; the ribbon is that of the GCVO. The Princess is also Patron of the Junior Red Cross in Great Britain, Canada, and Australia. Photograph by Cecil Beaton (Camera Press).

A romantic study of Princess Alexandra by Norman Parkinson (Camera Press).

Angus Ogilvy and his son James preparing to sail at Cowes on the Isle of Wight.
Photograph by Tim Graham.

(*opposite*) Princess Alexandra at home with her family in the garden of Thatched House
Lodge in Richmond Park, Surrey. James was sixteen and Marina fourteen when
photographed in 1980 by Patrick Lichfield (Camera Press).

Princess Alexandra with Lady Diana Spencer at Ascot shortly before her marriage to
H.R.H. Prince Charles in 1981. Photograph by Tim Graham.

were her friends. Nor would she let etiquette get in the way; to please them she cut the cake with a paper knife which she had been given. Even this small present was the result of her thoughtfulness. The pensioners had wanted each to save a shilling a week, but Alexandra, aware that this was a considerable sum in 1957, had insisted that this was more than they could really afford. Instead the amount they raised bought not only the paper knife, but a cut glass gum pot, and she accepted it with heartfelt thanks, telling them how she dealt with much of her own correspondence, and telling the delighted residents that she would use the gum pot for sticking on her own stamps.

Alexandra's popularity in her own village was also marked by an invitation from the Iver branch of the Women's Institute to become a member. Alexandra was happy to accept an enrolment card from the President, who amused the company of ladies by telling them that when she approached the Princess about membership, Her Royal Highness had replied 'I thought that Women's Institutes were for old ladies.' Amid the subsequent laughter, it was a smiling Alexandra who also received a leather-bound dictionary. Her acceptance of the membership was not simply a polite gesture, for Alexandra would often attend the meetings before her marriage, although as she ruefully told the President, nothing would improve her standard of cooking.

After the birthday celebrations, Alexandra resumed her nursing career. But that soon lost its novelty for the press, interest in the Princess switched to her dancing, for it was discovered that Alexandra often used to go to several quiet night clubs. Inevitably, now that she was twenty-one, eager spies watched to see if she favoured any particular partner. If she did, Alexandra was certainly not going to tell the press. However, what they lacked in details, reporters willingly provided in fiction. This sort of speculation, was nothing new to Alexandra. As early as 1955, when the Princess was only eighteen, an American columnist had made the blunder of the year when he announced that Alexandra 'would shortly marry Prince Herolde [sic] of Norway'. Not only was the spelling of Prince Harald's name completely wrong, but when nothing could be confirmed from Scandinavia, hopeful attention was turned instead to Greece, but again disappointment followed when Alexandra appeared to show no affection, apart from a family one, for the Crown Prince Constantine.

Before long, however, the reporters received a new morsel in the shape of a burglary incident from the car of David Bailey, a young friend of Alexandra. They lost no time in stretching it as far as it would go, and soon tongues were wagging.

During some days off from the hospital, the Princess had spent a weekend in London with friends, among them Bailey, a grandson of Lady Airlie, former Lady-in-Waiting to Queen Mary. The young man had taken Alexandra to his parents' house in Notting Hill for midnight coffee, and when the couple returned to the car, they were shocked to discover that Alexandra's cases were missing. After some investigation a police trap was laid, and the culprit was caught trying to retrieve the goods from a left luggage office at London Bridge Station. Luckily for Alexandra, the items of jewellery and other valuables that had been taken were recovered, and eventually the thief was given a six-month sentence. But that was where her good luck ended – soon all London was talking.

In some respects Bailey seemed a likely candidate for Alexandra's hand. The son of a rich glass manufacturer, he was an ex-guards officer, and although a commoner, he had the most important quality of discretion, for he never spoke in public about any meetings with the Princess. The fact that he was a grandson of Lady Airlie was given exaggerated importance, for so was Mr Angus Ogilvy, whom the Princess had known since 1955 but whose name was never linked with hers publicly. Not once did the press guess where Alexandra's feelings lay, and this was partly due to strict protocol rules. If the Princess had to be seen in public, she had to attend in a party of usually eight, and even if she knew the host she had to be seen to be greeted by him formally, as if they were meeting for the first time. But these advantages were little protection against the tireless efforts of the reporters. Alexandra became weary of the endless newspaper reports about whom she was supposed to be in love with, and once remarked to a friend, 'I don't know why everybody is marrying me off. After all, Mummy didn't marry until she was twenty-eight. There is plenty of time.'

This constant public exposure had far-reaching effects. After an attack of glandular fever during Easter, 1958, Alexandra decided not to resume her nursing training, for it seemed pointless to continue with a career that she now saw she could never fulfil. Ruefully, she admitted that she was not much good at it anyway, and joked that she was always afraid of dropping the baby on its head, but in fact Alexandra had done as well as any other trainee nurse, and was in many respects sorry to leave.

The experience gained at the hospital had been invaluable, and would serve her well in the future. Perhaps the greatest lesson was the insight it gave the Princess into the direction of her own future. If she had not attempted nursing, she would have always regretted not taking the chance, but now she could accept that she could fulfil herself as a member of the royal family, on her own terms, and using her own special abilities.

The time Alexandra had given to nursing had also helped her to overcome the occasional moments of awkwardness which had in the past been so carefully noted by the press. A few weeks after she left the hospital, Alexandra travelled to Manchester to open the City Art Gallery, and the engagement was a demonstration of her complete assurance. Any 'amateurishness' had gone, to be replaced by a completely professional, though never heartless approach. Wearing an attractive two-piece oatmeal suit and a turquoise toque, she delivered a speech in which every word was audible to all her audience. When the mayor rose to thank the Princess, he added, 'beauty is always welcome at our gallery'. Alexandra was pleased enough to blush.

Monotonous as the ceaseless rounds of tree planting, guard inspection and foundation-stone-laying must have been, it was all undertaken with a professional understanding of the importance of her role, and a total grasp of the qualities needed. What constantly surprised the organizers involved with her functions, however, was Alexandra's ability not simply to appear interested, but genuinely to be interested in those she met. Her crooked smile, inherited from Marina, helped those who regarded meeting royalty as an ordeal to feel relaxed and at ease. One other bonus was her remarkable memory. Once, when at an old people's home, she asked an old lady if they hadn't met before. 'Yes,' was the reply, 'I used to be a cleaner at Coppins.' It was helpful in making those Alexandra met feel that they were special, and had been singled out to feel important, perhaps for just once in their lives. Professional skill and natural character were blended as one.

# 9

# *Roving Ambassador*

ALEXANDRA'S SUCCESS HAD not gone unnoticed at Buckingham Palace, and little time was wasted in placing her in the front rank of royalty as far as her duties were concerned. In consultation with the government, it was decided that she should accompany Marina for a Latin American tour. Originally planned for a fortnight, taking in just Brazil and Chile, it was extended to five weeks when it was learned that Alexandra would share her mother's engagements. Alexandra, professional to a tee, immediately set to reading as much as possible about the countries she would visit, a habit she was never to lose. She knew how important it was to familiarize herself with local geography and custom, if she were to fulfil her duties properly, and it was something which particularly impressed her cousin Prince Philip.

While the ladies were preparing for the visit, their minds were taken up with Edward, who had fallen in love with Miss Katharine Worsley, of Hovingham Hall in Yorkshire. Impulsive in all his actions, the Duke of Kent wanted to marry Katharine at once, a wish only confirmed by the knowledge that he was to be posted to Germany by his regiment, the Royal Scots Greys. Marina, like many a mother in her position, felt that at the age of twenty-two Edward must show more caution and insisted that he wait.

Marina recommended that her Edward should serve his two years in Germany before deciding finally on his choice of bride, and Edward reluctantly accepted the advice. But matters were settled amicably. Alexandra quickly became friends with Miss Worsley, for they shared many interests, and her brother's bride-to-be had even worked with children in a home which had been founded by the Worsley family.

Early in March 1959 a Bristol Britannia 312 took Marina and Alexandra, now with their minds at rest, to their first stop in Mexico City. Even the arrival itself was something of a triumph. Alexandra stepped down the gangway in a pale blue silk dress, complemented by

Marina's choice of brilliant royal blue with a white floral hat. The colour obviously delighted the waiting crowds, and as Marina and Alexandra made their way to the official car over five hundred newspaper men jostled to get a closer look. The Kents drove at once to the National Palace, after a short rest at the British Embassy, and as a formal greeting, Marina invested the President on behalf of the Queen with the Knight Commander of the Grand Cross of St Michael, being honoured in return along with Alexandra with the investiture of the Order of the Aztec Eagle.

As neither Alexandra nor Marina spoke Spanish, Alexandra's speech of thanks was read by the Head of the American Department of the Foreign Office, the Honourable Henry Hankey, who had travelled with the Kents from England as an adviser on the more practical aspects of the visit, which included efforts to revive the trade links between Britain and South America which had lapsed during the Second World War. As roving ambassadors, it was hoped that the Kents would boost the flagging trade figures.

Their engagements included a visit to a Mexican rodeo, where the dazzling feats of horsemanship delighted an appreciative Alexandra. For the rodeo she wore a Mexican stole in bright lilac shades which had been given to her by the President's wife, a gesture which ensured her popularity in the eyes of the Mexicans.

Another evening Marina, dressed in old gold, appeared with Alexandra at a charity ball in aid of the blind, but again the young Princess was the star attraction in her blue floral patterned dress. She was in constant demand as a dancing partner, but the organizers of the function had thoughtfully provided her with a law student, to prevent the Princess from being mobbed. It was a glittering social affair, and more besides, as the presence of the Kents helped to raise over £15,000.

Alexandra was beginning to outshine even her mother, now fifty-two, in appearance, but typically she would not sit back and enjoy the new fame. It was during the South American tour that Marina came to appreciate the friendly support that her daughter gave her. Now in her prime, Alexandra was an ideal companion, always bright and cheerful, and ready to share the inevitable strain of such an arduous tour. Many considered that Alexandra had an understanding of her mother which went beyond her years, and seemed at times to be more of a sister than a daughter. Gone were the days when Marina felt compelled to watch her daughter with a strict eye, and issue instructions quietly in French.

Now the inspiration was in the other direction, and at Teotihuachan, Marina surprised onlookers by announcing that she intended to climb the 220 feet high pyramid. When asked if she was sure she could manage, the reply came, 'I am not as old as all that!'

The royal party now moved South. In Peru, a visit to Cuzco, famous for its ancient architecture, had to be cancelled because of a rail strike, but the mayor of the city refused to be disappointed, and flew to meet the Kents in Lima. He presented Marina with a silver mace, and Alexandra with a set of hand-embroidered robes, similar in design to those worn by a princess of the Ancient Aztec Court. Alexandra happily donned them and, just as she won Mexican hearts by wearing local dress as if it were her own, the exotic cheerful photographs which appeared in the press only increased her popularity further.

Wherever Alexandra travelled in South America she was followed by hordes of cameramen and press reporters. Her popularity had already reached Chile by the time the Kents visited the country as the last part of their tour. While they were dining with the British ambassador and the President, Alexandra asked the cause of the shouting and jubilation she could hear in the main street outside. Of course Alexandra could not understand the language, and was genuinely astonished to learn that the crowd was shouting its admiration of her. The following evening, when a crowd gathered outside the Moneda Palace in Santiago, again roaring for Alexandra, the President led her and Marina on to the balcony that overlooked the packed square to acknowledge the cheers. It was an emotional moment for Alexandra, who could not believe that at only twenty-two she could be the object of such admiration.

Such was the excitement caused by the Kents' visit that one report claimed that a crowd in Brasilia, tired of the over-zealous bodyguards who protected Alexandra, had thrown them into a nearby swimming pool. In fact the Princess had been the victim of a stomach upset and had not even visited the city, but the currency of the story was indicative of the almost fever-pitch interest in Alexandra.

Of course the tour was full of interest for Alexandra too – she would never forget the Andes or the Argentinian swamps she flew over. Nevertheless, her main reaction on coming home must have been one of fatigue, even for somebody used to hard work. But if she had questioned the value of such visits, where the hand-shaking and politeness might have bored somebody less resilient, Alexandra could at least be cheered by a newspaper report which read, 'The tireless Kents have done their part of the job. Now it's up to the City and to British businessmen to follow up the advantages they have created. The keys are in the door.' As a final vindication of the success of her tour, trade figures did indeed improve, just as had been hoped.

The visit had helped to impress upon Alexandra that her position carried an important practical value. The hint of rebelliousness against her situation which had occasionally broken through in previous years was now put aside. Alexandra was slowly discovering that it was possible to do what was expected of her and, at the same time, still express her own personality. In this way, she developed her own 'style'. She made amusing off-the-cuff-remarks, often quite unorthodox, and after the triumph of South America was the natural choice for Buckingham Palace to send on a tour of Australia later that year. But there was one important difference. It was decided that Alexandra was ready and capable of making the visit on her own.

# 10

# *Australian Triumph*

AUSTRALIA HAD ALWAYS enjoyed an important place in the Commonwealth, but in 1959, the traditional strong loyalty for the crown was being questioned by some younger Australians, who felt that their comparatively young country had little to gain from a distant and cloistered group of dignitaries. This, combined with the Australians' reputation for disliking pomposity and unnecessary starchiness, made the question of whom to send on the planned tour from Britain a sensitive one. As it happened, Princess Alexandra was ideal: her youthfulness and unstuffy demeanour would establish an instant rapport with the Australians, and do much to renew an interest in the royal family. It was an important task, and one which required particular qualities.

The very thought of touring such a large continent alone was an intimidating one for Alexandra. There was a list of nearly a hundred engagements to be undertaken in five weeks, and when the schedule was announced, the press gloomily predicted that the visit was bound to be a failure. It did seem that Alexandra was overburdened with functions and, as in the earlier Canadian tour, there was also criticism that she would be suffocated by unnecessary protocol, and be kept from those who wanted to see her.

The controversy had begun before the Princess even left her own country, and the difficult atmosphere threatened to wreck the tour before it got off the ground. So seriously was the criticism regarded that Alexandra was advised to call a news conference in London for over twenty Australian pressmen. The Princess asked that her remarks could be kept 'off the record', and once a relaxed meeting was established, she proved to be very much in control. She told reporters that she was taking the visit very seriously, because 'the tour is mainly concerned with the Queensland Centenary celebrations, so I mustn't play the giddy goat'. Before long her calmness and her grasp of the problems facing her, had persuaded the press that with Alexandra in charge the tour would be a success.

Nevertheless, the remark did not deter the reporters from asking the Princess their usual frivolous questions:

'Princess, why are you taking two swim suits?'

'It's just in case the other gets wet. Besides, I can't wear both on the Great Barrier Reef,' Alexandra replied adroitly.

'Have you been warned the warmer sea may shrink the material?' another reporter asked.

'Oh, will it?' Alexandra continued. 'In that case, I shall have to do some slimming as well as swimming.'

Many doubts about the tour had been removed, and the Australian government, who had been well aware of the criticism, responded by deciding that the accent of the tour would be on youth and on the number of young people invited to each function.

Great care had been taken with Alexandra's wardrobe, for she had to appear cool and smart in the Australian climate. Victor Stiebel designed several evening gowns, which, as often, incorporated some of Alexandra's own ideas, and Leslie King produced over twenty day dresses, including a wattle yellow one for Alexandra to wear when she arrived in Australia.

But the criticism also had some adverse effects. The Mayor of Queensland hastily extended the number of dances planned when he heard that he was accused of over-organizing the formalities of Alexandra's visit, something which not only increased the problems for Alexandra but did not even do away with the protocol. The committees who planned the balls were involved in endless discussion in trying to decide which of the young men in their towns was respectable enough to dance with their special visitor!

At last, after the seemingly endless preparations, Alexandra took off from London. Although touring without Marina was worrying, Alexandra was of course not without support. With her, apart from her Lady-in-Waiting and her doctor, was Mr Philip Hay, her mother's Private Secretary, whose experience and help could always be relied on to smooth over any potential problems. The party journeyed via Canada, and arrived fresh and relaxed at Canberra airport after a week's holiday en route in Fiji and Hawaii. The wattle-coloured dress, which Alexandra had carefully selected as a compliment to her host country delighted the Australians who arrived to greet her. But some were appalled that an immediate forest of hands waited to grasp hers, and worried that Alexandra would be suspicious of the boisterous pop-star welcome.

But they underestimated the Princess. Naturally she dined with the Prime Minister, Sir Robert Menzies, and had to attend numerous other functions which took place behind closed doors. But whenever possible, she would go out to meet the people. Even so, the Australians who were desperate for a glimpse of the Princess complained that she was being kept from them, but Alexandra was only taking a rest.

Their patience was soon rewarded, however, and after the first government ball, during which Alexandra was presented with a diamond brooch by Sir Robert Menzies, she appeared on a balcony, as in South America, in response to the excited shouts of 'We want Alexandra.'

From the start of the tour, Alexandra managed to gauge intuitively the feelings of the crowd who lined the city streets and the roads in the country. If she had kept to the usual code of behaviour normally followed by royalty, her visit would have been interesting, but nothing more than that. As it was, Alexandra realized that for Australia she had to contribute something new. When she wandered off on her own to take photographs, the press followed her through muddy fields, but at first slightly suspicious that she was leading them a merry dance. But soon they were convinced that this independence was as heartening as it was novel. Noticing Alexandra breaking out on unplanned routes of her own choice persuaded them that she would have liked more freedom than she was given, and through the early part of the tour, when the formal aspect of the visit was the most apparent, the Australians gratefully sensed that the Princess was on their side. It was something which was proved to be more than a belief.

Noticing the silent and rather awestruck faces that met her wherever she travelled, Alexandra would break the ice by suddenly moving away from her official party, and walking towards the crowd. Quite without any prompting, she chatted to various people, strolling about casually and smiling encouragement. It was an experiment which she repeated again and again, and one which was to prove more successful than she could imagine. Since dubbed 'the royal walkabout', it has been forgotten that it was Alexandra who started this now accepted and standard ingredient of royal visits.

Other people connected with the tour were less enthusiastic.

Officials wondered how royalty could cope with the problem of having to talk to any working man they might meet, for instance, and they were also worried about the added security problems. The crowds, however, had no such doubt about the effectiveness of Alexandra's friendly gesture. On that first day in Queensland, she made herself many friends, sensing the Princess's infectious good humour, the spectators echoed the phrase 'Welcome to Queensland' along the route as Alexandra drove to Brisbane.

The success of the walkabout was so much in tune with the new image of royalty that it was soon taken up by other members of the royal family. It was a democratic move, which accepted that the people who had come to welcome royalty were not just staring masses to be cordoned off at a safe distance, but people who could meet and talk to the visiting dignitaries.

The wild enthusiasm of Alexandra's admirers sometimes brought unfortunate results, as the National Agricultural Show in Brisbane, where many events celebrating the Queensland centenary were held. The moment Alexandra arrived, she was cheered by a vast throng who surged forward to meet her, stirring up clouds of dust in the dry heat. Lady Moyra, separated in the commotion, was anxious for Alexandra's safety, and some children were knocked over, but a moment or so later, Alexandra was helped through the crowds, with Lady Moyra once again at her side.

It was alarming while it lasted, but provided a lesson on safety which was taken up a few days later at a wood-chopping event to which Alexandra had been invited. This time Alexandra, whose visit was unannounced, entered the grounds by a side door.

Perhaps 'unexpected' was the keynote of Princess Alexandra's visit, for nearly everything she did surprised people. Whether it was simply grasping an old man's hand in a war veteran's home, or steering her launch on a zig-zag course to be near those who waited on the river bank to wave to her, her ideas always gave great pleasure. Inevitably, though, the relaxed emphasis that Alexandra placed on her visit gave officials some headaches. Her unprecedented action of stopping her car to pick up sometimes as many as twenty bouquets meant that the royal party did sometimes arrive late for engagements in the early stages of the tour. In answer to complaints about this, Alexandra brightly suggested that the pilot car should collect the flowers, for she was determined not to disappoint anyone.

The most publicized event of Alexandra's tour, was the 'affair of the top hat', circulated in the press to the point of boredom but a perfect example nevertheless of a small incident demonstrating the refreshing naturalness of Alexandra.

When she was leaving Brisbane Cathedral, after morning service, she walked with the Governor-General to speak to some of the cathedral choir members. Waving and smiling, she managed to return to her waiting car on the wrong side, and as she clambered in, promptly sat on the Governor-General's top hat, completely crushing it. Her accident had been witnessed by too many people to cover it up, and in earlier years, the Princess would have been mortified with embarrassment. Now, however, she made a feature of it, and turned the incident to her advantage, taking the hat and waving it to the crowd. She was greeted with a roar of sympathetic laughter as she drove off with the Governor-General nursing his battered hat.

The exhausting tour continued, with the pressmen always in tow. Alexandra did not let them bother her. She was aware that they were only doing their job, and genially referred to them as 'Alexandra's Rag-time Band'. Realizing that it was important to co-operate with them, she would always speak to new arrivals, and gained herself a good name among the reporters. Not only were the press and camera crew given encouragement – someone told the Princess that her faithful but often unnoticed drivers and baggage carriers were having a party, and she invited herself to it, staying for over two hours. Her energy seemed limitless, and those who worked for her were astonished at her vitality in the hot Australian climate.

If she inspired loyalty from her entourage by her example, she also made many new fans through her thoughtfulness. When a small girl was seen miles from anywhere waiting under a eucalyptus tree for Alexandra's car, quite alone and looking rather forlorn, the Princess stopped her car to speak to her young admirer, and to hand her a bar of chocolate.

Her flair for the right touch came from a natural desire to give pleasure. Young farmers jokingly tried to date Alexandra in Canberra, and thought that the matter ended there. Yet, to their astonishment, they later received tickets for a ball that evening, sent to them by Alexandra, who had not forgotten. After dancing half the night away, the Princess invaded the Governor-General's house, and fried bacon and eggs for her friends in the kitchen.

It was not just Alexandra's thoughtfulness in tactfully kissing koala bears which endeared her to Australians, for all that had been done before by visiting royalty. What made her visit special was not even the 'top hat affair', but her genuine interest in all she saw, rather than the usual polite approving nod. More than anything else, this was appreciated by those who had gone to considerable trouble to organize the events.

Not that everything went smoothly. There were moments of distinct embarrassment for onlookers, even if Alexandra betrayed nothing but her cheerful smile. At Rockhampton, she had to endure a poor display of amateur dancing, in which everything went completely wrong. Later at Brisbane, while Alexandra was receiving an honorary degree, she was quite unperturbed when confronted by a student dressed as a pineapple.

It was the frequent moments of amusement and warmth that made the arduous tour such a joy. The culmination of the happiness she gave the Queenslanders was expressed by 65,000 schoolchildren in a mass demonstration of cheering for the Princess as she left Brisbane. She had made the centenary celebrations unforgettable, and had won a place in the Australians' hearts, which she still retains.

Later, in Sydney, 'Alexandra fever' reached its pitch at the University Women's College. Chants of 'We want Alex' roared from the students and in their enthusiasm to greet her they knocked the Princess's hat off. This time, the surprise fancy-dress guest was a male student in a white ballet costume and army boots, who clearly amused Alexandra as he handed her some flowers. With a 'Thank you, they're lovely', she tried to enter the Women's College, but was prevented by the students who wanted to accompany her. The police forced them back, an unpopular move which provoked the students to respond by letting down the tyres of the police vehicles and showering the policemen themselves with pennies and water bombs. The rumpus did not die down, and when Alexandra tried to leave the university the police had to force a passage to let her car through, receiving a few punches from the students in the process.

The fanatically intense response aroused by Alexandra's appearance at the university was similiar to the behaviour now familiar at pop concerts, but then it was unheard of that anyone, let alone visiting royalty, could ever arouse such passion. It was not surprising that some of the strain on Alexandra resulted in laryngitis, and she was obliged to cancel some of her functions.

Amidst all the noisy jubilation, an important and symbolic expression of loyalty came from Australia's oldest inhabitants, the Aborigines. She was taken to see a corroboree, an Aboriginal story-telling performance involving singing and dancing. The Aborigines, people who often regarded white Australians as intruders in their own land, gave Alexandra a dignified and sincere welcome. Instead of the usual rugs, jewels or flowers, the seventy-seven-year-old leader handed the Princess a simple boomerang to round off a delightful day. He had obligingly put on a pair of pants to greet Alexandra, and she much enjoyed the entertainment.

This both summed up the complete success of the tour, both for the Australians and for Alexandra. Driving through Melbourne for the last time, Alexandra made no attempt to keep back the tears of emotion as she was regaled with deafening cries of 'Come back, Alex! Come back soon!' No one doubted her word when she said, in Melbourne, 'I must come back, for I have loved it all.'

After the Princess left Darwin for a few days in Cambodia on her way home to London, an Australian women's magazine summed up popular opinion about the impression Alexandra had created in Australia.

Princess Margaret should marry an American to bind Old England and the United States of America together. And we'll have Alexandra out here. She can marry one of us. They shouldn't all be piled up in England.

More realistically, another reporter from Australia commented,

The wonderful performance of our up and coming Princess has done so much to put a zestful face on the old country in the past five weeks.

The Australian tour was a personal triumph for Alexandra, and her success removed any doubts she had about her own ability to carry out duties efficiently. Perhaps, unwittingly, she had made royal history by her innovation of the walkabout, and, more importantly, had developed a personality which would soon make her known as 'the popular Princess'.

# 11

# *Rumours of Romance*

ALEXANDRA'S TRIUMPHANT HOMECOMING, marked by a dinner and dance given by a grateful Queen and the Duke of Edinburgh at Buckingham Palace, was to confront her with new developments in which gossip would inevitably involve her. While Alexandra had been abroad, Princess Margaret had been observed to have taken a leaf out of her cousin's book by appearing unexpectedly radiant when undertaking engagements in Glasgow. In fact, Princess Margaret had another reason for being happy, for she was in love with Anthony Armstrong-Jones, and the well-kept secret was only made public on 26 February 1960, when their engagement was announced. Anthony Armstrong-Jones was one of the guests present at the celebratory dinner for Alexandra, and he looked as happy as his fiancée.

Only six years separated Princess Margaret and Alexandra, and in many respects they shared a streak of self-willed independence which had at one time drawn them together. Alexandra had sympathized intensely with her cousin, and the personal unhappiness she had suffered in having to renounce the friendship of Group-Captain Peter Townsend. Princess Elizabeth's engagement to Philip Mountbatten had only emphasized the impossible situation between Margaret and Townsend, and for some time Margaret subsequently felt cool towards Prince Philip, whose extrovert personality contrasted so strongly with the artistic Townsend. But other factors had severed this friendship. Margaret had also resented the way in which Marina had encouraged the entry of her compatriot Philip into the royal circle and was concerned that this older coldness might interfere with the latest events. Marina had strong views on the image of royalty, and also had a number of friends who touched on the artistic society of which Armstrong-Jones was part: Margaret was well aware that Marina might have learnt some interesting trifle against Armstrong-Jones which she could now use to influence her ally Prince Philip, and thus the Queen.

This problem arose because under the Marriage Act the Queen's consent was required for any marriage that Margaret might wish to contract. Understandably, Margaret was determined to prevent any obstacles being raised against her marriage, and was careful about how she broke the news. First, she told Queen Elizabeth, the Queen Mother, and only then the Queen with the instruction not to tell Philip until he was in a good mood.

Marina was told about the impending engagement only a few days before the official announcement, when it was impossible for her to do anything about it. When she had time to consider the news, all she could do was to complain to various guests, including Nöel Coward, about the unsuitability of Margaret's choice.

The malicious storm of abuse that blew up when it was learned that the Queen's sister was to marry a commoner contrasted with the entirely favourable press that Alexandra was now receiving. Unfortunately the press tactlessly insisted on comparing her behaviour with the selfless attitude that Alexandra gave to her duties and for which she was now becoming famous.

Now that Margaret was engaged, press attention inevitably turned to Alexandra as the next eligible princess. Alexandra refused to give out any secrets, and kept the press guessing, however, and so the papers had to resort to a fortune-teller's prediction that she would 'almost certainly become engaged in 1963. Her future will be linked with a European Royal House, and even a throne. She will marry a man who is sensitive both in physique and character, a retiring personality. . . . Their marriage will be a success . . . she will quickly have children of both sexes. . . .'

Alexandra may well have smiled when she read the prediction, for as she was really only devoted to Angus Ogilvy at least some of the points mentioned were correct. None of that was known outside her immediate family, however, and the press had to latch on to anything for clues. The Princess often paid private visits to Baronscourt, the home of Lady Moyra Hamilton, for instance, and there would meet Moyra's brother the Marquess of Hamilton. The reporters were happy to speculate, especially as he was often noticed at parties with Alexandra.

Also there was his friend, Lord O'Neill, who was considered a more likely match, even though he only very remotely fitted the fortune-teller's choice, being descended from the ancient Kings of Ireland. Three years older than Alexandra, he lived in Shane Castle in

Co. Tyrone, and when Alexandra was due to travel to Ireland in 1959, Lord O'Neill was asked about any possible romance with the Princess, and whether an engagement was imminent. He was reported as re-marking that 'it's all in the air', and consequently Alexandra cancelled her travel plans across the Irish Sea. Several months later, Raymond O'Neill was questioned again, and this time confused everyone by replying, 'There is no question of an engagement. I am what's called "fancy free". We're just good friends and that happens to be the truth.'

Nevertheless, speculation continued, and when Alexandra was seen with the Irish peer in a fashionable restaurant, and they even danced together, much was made of it. The rumours only increased when O'Neill dined at Coppins with Marina the following month, and all the denials were quickly ignored.

But of course, Alexandra's marriage was a serious issue too, in the family especially. In the past, Marina hoped that Alexandra would marry a foreign prince, and with this in mind the young princess had been introduced to a variety of possible royal suitors over the years. In March 1960, for example, she spent a weekend with the Swedish Royal family at a house party given by King Gustav in honour of his three eldest grand-daughters. Alexandra was photographed with Crown Prince Harald of Norway, but the press interest once again centred on Crown Prince Constantine of Greece, four years younger than Alexandra and then serving in the Royal Navy. Marina would have welcomed a match between him and her daughter, as it would have strengthened the ties between the Greek and British thrones, but disappointment followed. Constantine flew into London with his mother and sister, but instead of joining her mother to meet them at the airport, Alexandra departed for a weekend at Baronscourt. It was clear, as it really always had been, that Alexandra had no romantic interest in her Greek cousin.

It might well have been argued that at that time Alexandra had little opportunity for romance, for her public engagements were beginning to keep her fully occupied. Following the success of Australia, it was announced that Alexandra would represent the Queen at the inde-pendence celebrations in Nigeria.

The visit was less arduous than the long Australian tour, and was only planned to last eight days, but it began ominously when, on 26 September 1960, Alexandra arrived in Lagos in torrential rain. For the Nigerians themselves, however, rain was the sign of an important visitor, and the smiling children greeting the Princess as she drove to

71

Government House confirmed the local interpretation of the weather. Remarkably, even though the route was crammed with people waiting to welcome her, Alexandra insisted on being driven in an open car. Her only concession to the weather was a light raincoat, and she stepped out of the vehicle soaking wet at the end of the journey.

The rain returned for an official garden party at Government House, and again Alexander refused to accept advice that she would be wiser to remain indoors. Bravely she squelched through the muddy garden, the rain even spreading the dye of her hibiscus pink hat down her face. This she ignored and it was only when the Governor-General, Sir James Robertson, who accompanied Alexandra, discovered that his own grey suit had turned black, that Alexandra was finally persuaded to take cover.

That same evening, Princess Alexandra appeared at a dance as cheerful as ever in a diamond tiara and a green ball gown. Nothing had dampened her spirits, and she danced for much of the night with her Nigerian equerry as though she had been resting all day.

At the Government House ball her keen ear picked up a West African dance called the 'High Life', a casual hip-swinging version of the quickstep. She was a skilful dancer, and her lightness on foot was only emphasized by the results of a crash diet she had undertaken before the visit. It would have been unfair to say that Alexandra was plump, but she readily admitted that at times she had to watch her figure. For six weeks before leaving for Nigeria, Alexandra had insisted on having no alcohol (she drinks very sparingly in any case), no fruit juice except lemon, and strictly prohibiting all sweets and cakes. Even what she did allow herself, small portions of fish and meat, would have daunted one with less strength of will.

Fortunately in Nigeria, that could all be forgotten, and happily the sun shone in a cloudless sky on the actual day that independence was granted. It was a moving moment as the British flag was lowered for the last time, and one which clearly upset the retiring Governor-General. Alexandra, now thoroughly experienced at public ceremony, tactfully smiled encouragement to him.

Alexandra, wearing a dress of shimmering white, then read the Queen's speech from the throne of the new Parliament House. Her voice echoed clearly and confidently round the chamber, and Alexandra further impressed the Prime Minister by identifying the various delegates present by their individual styles of African dress, the result of her usual diligent preparation. She continued to impress her hosts as the tour progressed – Alexandra opened new sports centres, visited universities and made countless other appearances, often in the rain which had greeted her.

During a State Banquet the princess, wearing a simple lotus pink dress, read a speech which she had written herself. She told the Nigerian ministers that she was

. . . going to say what I feel. It is something of an experience to see Africa for the first time in one's life, and I do not imagine that the opportunity is given to many people of my age, to visit so important, so respected and so typical a part of Africa as this. During the few days I have spent with you, I have enjoyed myself. . . .

Although such foreign visits were always characterized by their serious intentions, there was always light relief when Alexandra was around. On one occasion she was taken to see the harem of the Emir of Bida in the north of the country. The Emir showed Alexandra round his palace, a building which housed over two hundred women and was understandably barred to all men, and then Alexandra was introduced to his 'official' four wives. Quite unable to tag along with the protocol, she found it hard to restrain a smile as the remainder were passed off as 'members of his family'.

There was time, too, to relax at the end of the busy tour, and a four-hour flight changeover in which she was expected to rest. Instead, at her typically energetic requests she was driven to see the Roman remains at Tripoli, a journey that took an hour and a half in all. When Alexandra finally arrived in London, she was met by Marina and the Earl of Scarborough, who represented the Queen.

Everyone was now saying that Alexandra was the princess who could never put a foot wrong, and for her unequalled service abroad, the Queen conferred on her the honour of the Dame of the Grand Cross of the Royal Victorian Order. The citation read that the order was awarded for having rendered 'extraordinary or important personal service to the Sovereign'. After the false starts of her early career, it was a gratifying tribute to the new 'star' of the royal family.

# 12

# *The Far East*

AFTER SO MUCH official foreign travel, Alexandra welcomed the chance to go abroad simply to enjoy a holiday, free from engagements. In the New Year of 1961 she was the guest of the King and Queen of Thailand in the Palace Hotel in Gstaad in Switzerland. The Princess had gone there for the ski-ing, which she adored, but her association with the monarch of Thailand threatened to be an embarrassment, as the king was coming under criticism and even received abusive letters complaining that while he and his Queen were living in luxury, his own subjects were suffering great poverty. They had in fact been away from their own country for the previous six months, and as part of their own celebrations they organized a Gala Ball, to which Alexandra was invited. Louis Armstrong was engaged to play there at great expense, and tickets were on sale at £12 10s. (£12.50), in those days a huge sum for such an event. The extravagance of the whole affair, of course, only invited further criticism of the King's neglect of his country.

Alexandra, aware of the hazards of the situation, diplomatically left the hotel the night before the ball was to take place. Many who had bought the expensive tickets simply to see Alexandra were furious when they discovered that she would not be there, and tried to recover their money. With this bad start, the Gala Ball was consequently a disaster, and no one was more disappointed than Louis Armstrong, who counted the Princess as one of his fans. 'What a shame that sweet little Princess Alexandra couldn't stay,' he said regretfully. 'I know she would have liked to hear me blow that horn.'

Back in Kensington Palace in the meantime there was excitement in quite a different direction. Edward had now completed his two years in Germany, and had decided quite firmly that he intended to marry Katharine Worsley. His engagement to the Yorkshire girl was announced early in March 1961, and it was planned that the wedding ceremony would take place not in Westminster Abbey, as might have been expected, but in Miss Worsley's favourite and home cathedral, York Minster. Unusual though it was for the bride to exercise her prerogative of choosing the place of marriage when it was a royal wedding, this decision did not create any extra problems.

In the meantime, there was a great deal of preparation to attend to, and Marina took in hand the important matter of the bride's dress. She suggested that Katharine should see the work of the designer who had given her and Alexandra so much pleasure, John Cavanagh. Cavanagh had, as a young man, been trained under Edward Molyneux, who had made Marina's own wedding dress twenty-seven years earlier. It was the first wedding in the close-knit Kent family since then, and the occasion must have aroused mixed feelings for Marina, who depended a great deal on her children for support. Only three weeks before the wedding ceremony, Marina emphasized this family solidarity and prepared herself for the momentous event to come when she travelled with Edward and Alexandra to pay tribute at the scene of the Duke of Kent's death. As before, they were driven in a Land-Rover along rough heather tracks, and as they made their slow climb to the simple, poignant cross, the police waited respectfully behind. There was no doubt that the visit was a symbolic one, and it could not but remind Edward of the duty he had inherited from his father, whom he resembled in so many ways.

When the day arrived, everything ran joyfully according to plan, except of course the weather, which was undecided between rain and bursts of bright sunshine. The Cavanagh wedding dress was noteworthy for its long train of satin-edged silk gauze and, surprisingly, the panel of veiling, fastened by diamond pins tucked under the headdress, which hid the bride's face. The extra veil was removed at the end of the ceremony, and as Miss Worsley made her way down the long nave of the ancient minster, in the spangled light of the great east window, the largest medieval stained-glass window in the world, it would have been difficult to have imagined a more romantic and moving sight.

Marina, as always perfectly dressed, wore a Cavanagh-designed outfit of champagne silk organdie, decorated with diamante and gold and silver thread, and topped by an enormous cartwheel-shaped hat of matching osprey feathers. Alexandra wore silk in azalea pink, with a close fitting toque of the same shade. Despite this splendour, the sight of her son, tall and handsome in the ceremonial uniform of his regiment, proved at times too much for Marina, and she looked nervous and strained. Alexandra, who always understood her mother, gave Marina the reassurance she needed, and by the time she returned from witnessing the register, they were both perfectly calm and composed. The new era which was beginning was masked by the announcement that she would no longer be styled the Duchess of Kent, but would revert to her original title of Princess Marina.

Happy as Alexandra was at the marriage of her brother, the constant obsession that the press had with her own future, which only increased with the event, must have been annoying, to say the least. Ludicrous suggestions that Alexandra might marry the ageing Shah of Persia could be laughed off privately, but speculation continued as long as there was no clue available about Alexandra's intentions. David Bailey's name had been removed after he announced his own engagement in September 1961, and this left Lord O'Neill as apparently the most likely choice, but he surprised the princess by remarking rather carelessly that he was the one who was

hesitating about marriage to Alexandra. I don't want to become like Philip, a prisoner of protocol. I don't want to be obliged to walk two steps behind my wife, clasping my hands behind my back like a clever little boy. Alexandra loves me very much, but I don't want Buckingham Palace as part of my dowry.

It was perhaps a timely reminder that a royal match was not every young man's ideal, but it did nothing to remove Lord O'Neill from the race for Alexandra's hand in the eyes of the press. Indeed, the interest continued during Alexandra's visit to the small Scottish island of Islay, later in the summer of 1961, as the guest of the owner, Mr Charles Morrison. Also there was Lord O'Neill, and the popular press confidently stated that their engagement would be announced soon. Moreover, it had been observed that before leaving for the island Lord O'Neill had bought an expensive ring from the same West End shop that had provided the Duke of Kent with his wedding ring.

It was true that Alexandra fuelled rumours by constantly being seen with Lord O'Neill. While the rest of the party was grouse shooting, Alexandra, wearing a chunky black pullover and tartan skirt, was seen walking hand in hand with the Irish peer. Later the couple were glimpsed enjoying a picnic together, still alone, apart from the royal romance watchers. But, much to everyone's disappointment, when the time came to leave Islay Alexandra's hand was as noticeably bare of rings as when she had arrived. But the reporters were undeterred – it was concluded that the engagement was actually decided but that as the Court was in mourning for an uncle of the Queen, Sir David Bowes-Lyon, it would be announced at a more suitable moment.

There was not a word of truth in the reports. In fact, it was not Lord O'Neill who had bought the ring in London, but Lord Ednam, who was about to remarry. Of much more importance for Alexandra than romance, or at least providing the press with details of one, was her fondness for trying new activities and travelling. She had a pleasant few days with the Duke of Edinburgh, who gave her sailing lessons on his yacht *Coweslip* at Cowes, and enjoyed a few private visits to Florence, Greece, and Scotland, before preparing for yet another royal tour, this time to the Far East.

At first it was intended that Alexandra should only visit Hong Kong in late 1961, but plans involving the princess had by now formed a habit of almost always altering because of her popularity, and this time Japan, Burma and Thailand had managed to find a place on her itinerary.

Alexandra's fame had travelled before her. In Hong Kong she was known as the *Ngar Lai Sun Kwun Tzu*, or the Princess Elegant and Beautiful Coral. British royalty was a relatively unfamiliar sight in Hong Kong, and, to make the tour even more of a challenge, the unusual customs and traditions of the Far East were new even to the much-travelled Alexandra. It was to be a test of her adaptability, but there were some familiar scenes. The pattern of cheering crowds and often over-enthusiastic pushing mobs she had come to know from visits to Australia and Nigeria was repeated in the area outside St John's Cathedral. As she left the service there, the Hong Kong children were delighted by her turquoise cotton suit and white felt hat, and surged forward to meet the princess. The police had to thrust Alexandra hurriedly into her car to prevent her from being crushed, and crowd control became a problem throughout the tour as Alexandra explored the markets and even managed a little water ski-ing.

Once again Alexandra earned herself huge popularity, but no one will remember her visit with greater affection than a Hong Kong dairy worker and his family, who lived on the fifteenth floor of a skyscraper. They had been asked to be hosts to Alexandra for afternoon tea, and were petrified with nerves at the prospect of receiving a British princess. For weeks before, they practised their bows and curtseys, but

Alexandra soon dispelled any awkward formalities, and her hosts were thrilled to discover her warm sense of humour and keen interest in what they had to say, which turned their feared ordeal into an unforgettable treat. After enjoying English biscuits and Indian tea with the family, Alexandra left to watch a children's rally. The dairy worker was so impressed with Alexandra's visit that he kept the cup she drank from complete with the added souvenir of a lipstick imprint, and his reports of the occasion only swelled Alexandra's popularity.

The original purpose of Alexandra's visit, and still its main event, was to attend the celebrations of the fiftieth anniversary of the University of Hong Kong. At an impressive ceremony, the Princess was honoured with the conferment of an honorary Doctorate of Law, but just as she was about to give a speech of thanks her cap slipped over her eyes. Cheers and laughter burst out, and when still blinded, Alexandra laughingly told her audience that she had 'always wanted to see Hong Kong'.

She continued to impress during the rest of the day. She was the guest of honour at a ten-course meal given by the government, which had to be eaten with chopsticks. The guests were not only surprised at her expertise with these difficult implements, but also with her efforts at the notoriously difficult Chinese language. She dismissed the praise with a modest, 'I've been practising in my bath every morning!', but of course it was not the joke it seemed, and hinted at the usual hard preparation.

Perhaps of equal importance to Alexandra was a visit she made to a centre which had been opened to give craftwork to blind Chinese refugees. No matter how harrowing she found such visits, Alexandra always conveyed an uplifting warmth and interest, even to those who could not see her.

Her unpredictable actions had long ceased to surprise her press party, who now dubbed her 'Alexandra the Greatest'. Particularly ardent in his attention towards the princess was Robert Haswell of the *Daily Express*, who would later shock the establishment by taking an official birthday photograph of her, something unprecedented for a Fleet Street photographer. When Alexandra was taken to Hong Kong's border with Communist China, she tried to take a photograph of some farm workers half a mile away in China itself. Her own camera was too small, and the *Mirror* photographer handed Alexandra his own camera with its long-focus lens. Alexandra did not intend to favour the *Mirror* with a photograph which they could present as taken by the princess, but while she was looking at the view with it, she did inadvertently take a photograph. At this the *Express* cameraman, Haswell, was far from happy, knowing that the *Mirror* man was already working out the fastest means by which he could send back his wonderful scoop, Alexandra's own photograph. It was a situation which Alexandra quickly grasped herself, and with her usual flair did the only thing possible. She borrowed Haswell's camera, and took another shot of China. Both newspapers sent her results by express post and they were printed with matching captions, 'The Picture Alex took'.

After Hong Kong, the tour continued with a visit to Japan. Diplomatically, the visit was an important one, being the first occasion since the war that Japan had received a member of the royal family of its recent enemy. This delicate situation demanded more from Alexandra than perhaps might even have been expected from anybody else, but she coped admirably, as usual, and there was no sense of embarrassment as Alexandra was greeted on her arrival at Tokyo by Princess Chichibu, Emperor Hirohito's sister-in-law, and the Prime Minister.

Alexandra had been warned about the strictness of etiquette in Japan, and how easy it was to cause offence without ever intending it. Being taller than most of her hosts, for instance, she had to be careful to avoid any reference to the small stature of the Japanese. She also had to avoid laughing openly, as Japanese etiquette interprets laughter in somebody's face as humour at their expense. Alexandra was naturally often amusing, and amused, and did not normally mind showing this side of her nature, but she had to restrain her lively spirits. Her temptation to laugh was never greater than when, in a Japanese temple, she tripped on a loose carpet. Her tiny guide was overcome with horror, and apologized over-profusely. It was a slightly ridiculous situation in which Alexandra quickly saw the humour, but as she recalled to a friend,

It was so terribly funny. After all, there was no need to apologize at all. Then I remembered being told about them being so desperately sensitive, and I just managed to keep a straight face.

Alexandra need hardly have worried, for her meticulous attention to detail impressed everybody, to the surprise of some. At a theatre, where she was loudly applauded, she waved to those who were in the cheapest seats at the top gallery. The Japanese, who would themselves have ignored this part of the audience, were as impressed as they were astonished, and hailed Alexandra with a newspaper caption which read 'The Pearl Princess greets the poor'.

The 'Pearl Princess', however, would not compromise her values simply to be diplomatic. When she was taken by the Crown Prince to witness duck-netting at Saitana, she refused to be photographed with a bird in a net with its wing already broken. Instead she insisted on setting an uninjured bird free and allowing photographs of that.

On a happier note, she was taken by the president of a large pearl company to watch divers searching for pearls. From a small boat, she saw the divers bob about with wooden tubs, which, if they were lucky, would surface with a few cultured pearls. Alexandra was kissed on her hands by lines of dripping wet divers, and really became the 'Pearl Princess' when she was given a string of pearls by her host.

After the endless tours through Japanese gardens, department stores, medical centres and official halls, there was still no rest for Alexandra on leaving Japan, as she was then the guest of the Prince and Princess of Thailand in Bangkok. On one occasion there, realizing the difficulty of the complicated language, the princess strolled over to her ever-faithful press team, handed them a piece of paper, and remarked, 'I've written the names down for your captions. Don't get them wrong!'

The press were still in sight when Alexandra arrived next at Burma for a nine-day visit at the end of November. The most spectacular sight there was the romantic Shwe Dayon Pagoda in Rangoon, a notable temple containing relics of three Buddhas. Positioned on a high hill, the many tiers of solid gold rose to a height twelve and a half feet taller than St Paul's Cathedral, and was a sight never forgotten by Alexandra, who visited it early in the morning, to catch the full splendour of the flashing gold. She spent an hour or so there, barefoot as the temple rules demanded, and was astonished to hear from her guide that the pagoda contained over twenty-five tons of gold and silver, added to once in every generation by private donations. Alexandra was so impressed by the beauty she saw that she left a generous cheque with the guardian of the building. Alexandra had chosen the right moment to visit the temple, for the mosquitos that plagued her for much of the visit were at their least conspicuous early in the day. They had been troublesome at times, but Alexandra joked, 'They like me because I'm sweet.'

After a visit to the Egyptian temples at the Aswan Dam, Alexandra returned from her long tour to a cold British winter day. A welcoming reception at Kensington Palace included members of Sir Alec Douglas-Home's government, who wished to thank the Princess for carrying out so well her diplomatic mission, another facet Alexandra had added to her versatile and professional capabilities.

# 13

# *Preparing to Wed*

ALTHOUGH ALEXANDRA WAS now being hailed as royalty's biggest success story, it was still not passing unnoticed that she would be twenty-five on Christmas Day 1961, and was the only member of her family undertaking such extensive engagements who remained unmarried.

At twenty-five, Alexandra could, if she wished, marry without the consent of the Queen, although under certain circumstances she would have had to renounce her place in succession to the throne if she did so. As far as the endless speculation was concerned, the various celebrations which Alexandra attended at the time were no help to anyone who was trying to guess where her affections lay. The silver wedding of Queen Juliana and Prince Bernhardt of the Netherlands, and then the wedding in Athens of Princess Sophie and Prince Juan Carlos, now King of Spain, which Alexandra also attended, were eagerly scanned by the matchmakers, but without success.

The truth was that Alexandra knew perfectly well that she wished to marry her long-standing friend the Hon. Angus Ogilvy, and for some time had had no doubts about her choice. But the build-up to the engagement illustrated perfectly the strengths and weaknesses of Alexandra's position. She knew only too well of the problems involved in marrying a commoner, difficulties illustrated by marriage between Lord Snowdon and Princess Margaret, many of which had arisen because of Lord Snowdon's desire to introduce a more relaxed style into the royal family. In that case, Lord Snowdon had learnt that his ideas of freedom and his private life with his wife could not always be realized, and Alexandra was sympathetic and consequently cautious.

Alexandra's position was rather different from Margaret's, however, having been spared to some extent the constant scrutiny to which her older cousin was subjected. This had made it easier for her to find her own personality, and live by it. Alexandra never made the mistake of rebelling too strongly against the unwritten royal code of behaviour. Margaret, on the other hand, had only harmed herself by such protests as wearing a mini skirt when inspecting troops and displaying a large Mickey Mouse watch on her wrist.

Because Alexandra had never attracted a bad press, she was not constantly watched for possible mistakes. She reserved her casual clothes for times when she was completely off duty, and occasionally was able to slip out of Kensington Palace quite unobserved to shop in the West End. One can imagine how well Alexandra must have understood Margaret's position, and her apparent longing for personal freedom. At least Alexandra could lunch with friends in Soho, or take a taxi and chat freely with the driver. This freedom in its turn brought its own benefits. When she once bumped her car into another vehicle, the driver was so astonished when he recognized the culprit that he found himself saying 'My fault entirely', even though his car had been stationary.

At times, Alexandra doubtless hankered after a more private life, but as she knew this was impossible and had learned to live happily with her situation. There was little doubt that whomever she did marry would not be chosen because he had any desire to enter the royal family; Alexandra was too much of a realist to wish to thrust the restricted life on one who did not truly love her for her own sake, and too honest to choose a husband for any reason other than love.

Her life style clearly indicated that she did not particularly relish the more glamorous aspects of her position, and her pleasure in doing simple things and mingling with the crowd could be gratified without fuss because, as a friend remarked, 'No one takes any notice, simply because they do not expect to see a princess doing such ordinary things.'

So although Alexandra's engagement to the Hon. Angus Ogilvy completely took the country by surprise when it was eventually announced, the revelation did not seem at all extraordinary to those who knew Alexandra well. The romance was not a whirlwind one, for they had first met at an Eton Beagles Ball eight years previously, and they had considered every aspect of the situation facing them before taking the plunge.

They were both aware of the possible problems such a marriage might cause, but during a house party at Queen Elizabeth the Queen Mother's home at Birkhall they finally made up their minds. The

Queen Mother knew of Alexandra's feelings, and the complexities facing the young couple, and tactfully arranged for her guests to leave Angus alone with Alexandra as much as possible. Together they talked over the possible objections, and realized that their mutual love was more important than anything else, and would enable them to overcome any problems. The first difficulty, of Angus being a commoner, had been helped by the precedence of Anthony Armstrong-Jones, now Lord Snowdon. It was well known too that Princess Marina had always hoped that her daughter would marry a prince, but in the end she was only concerned for Alexandra's happiness, and would support whatever her daughter really wanted.

Ogilvy was no stranger to the royal family, as several of his relations had been courtiers; most recently his father, who had been Lord-in-Waiting to the late George V, and was Lord Chamberlain to the Queen Mother. In addition, his grandmother, Lady Airlie, was a Woman of the Bedchamber to Queen Mary, and had been one of her closest friends. Angus therefore knew the royal scene very well, and had no illusions about what faced him. Nevertheless, he was afraid that Marina would consider him unsuitable because he came from a family which was far from rich, and he had to earn his living in the City as a businessman. Before graduating from Oxford, with a degree in Modern Greats (philosophy, politics and economics), Angus had spent some time in the army, where he qualified as a ski-instructor. It was then he suffered a bad accident, which not only damaged a knee cap, but left him with a permanent back injury, which would cause him pain throughout his life.

When Ogilvy finally asked for Alexandra's hand, Marina gave no instant decision, but instead invited Angus to dinner at Kensington Palace. Rather disconcertingly, a secretary later asked him to arrive an hour earlier than he had originally arranged, but once at the Palace he was relieved to hear from Alexandra that all was well.

Angus insisted from the beginning that if he married Alexandra, he intended to continue with his work in the City. He required his job for his main source of income, something encouraged by Marina, as Alexandra would only be granted a small allowance at her marriage.

The Queen was also delighted to give her approval to the marriage, and there remained only the question of the reaction of Lord and Lady Airlie, Angus's parents. A friend close to the family has said that his parents saw all the snags, and felt he was marrying out of his class. After all, they took the old-fashioned view that royals marry royals. They were completely realistic about the situation, but of course they were very fond of Alexandra, and while they might have preferred not, they were only concerned that both Alexandra and their son should be happy. It was ironic, for his family had fought the Hanoverians for many years.

Any final doubts were removed when Lord and Lady Airlie and other members of their family dined with the Kents on 20 November. Alexandra was overjoyed, and decided to announce her engagement on her mother's wedding anniversary, 29 November 1962.

For a few days before the inevitable press hunt began, Alexandra relaxed quietly with Angus on a motoring holiday in England, exploring the countryside, stopping at pubs, and even visiting transport cafés for bacon and eggs. Alexandra disguised herself with headscarf and glasses, and as Angus was completely unknown to the public, they went about unrecognized.

The news of their engagement was made official at 5.15, and the statement from Kensington Palace read,

It is with the greatest pleasure that Princess Marina, Duchess of Kent, announces the betrothal of her daughter Princess Alexandra, to Angus Ogilvy, second son of the Earl and Countess of Airlie, to which the Queen has gladly given her consent.

Several members of both families had been sworn to strict secrecy about the engagement, including Iain Tennant, Angus's brother-in-law, and a fellow director of Scottish Grampian television. He was engaged in a board meeting there on the afternoon in question, and had been questioned by the other directors who were puzzled by Ogilvy's absence. Tennant resisted the questions until a few minutes after 5.15, when he glanced at his watch and said, 'I have to apologize for the absence of Mr Angus Ogilvy. He is going to marry Princess Alexandra. I think that concludes the business of the day, gentlemen.'

There was no doubt of the obvious pleasure the couple felt when they posed for the engagement photographs, in which the Princess proudly displayed her ring, a large sapphire supported on each side by a diamond. She told everyone that she was 'very, very happy', and that it was a relief, after keeping her secret for so long a time, to be able to come out in the open and to share her joy with friends.

Despite the fact that Angus was unknown to the public, it could be surmised that he shared at least some of Alexandra's views of her own place in the royal family. He had emphatically stated that he wished to remain in the background, and would never be tempted to use his entry into the royal family for any gain or advantage. Understandably, the first impression he made on the press was a favourable one. He was seen as a quiet businessman who had happened to fall in love with a princess of the royal family, and, as friends have often said, he saw this as more of a disadvantage than otherwise.

There had never been any doubt in Angus's mind or his family's that he would have to earn his keep. Although he came from a titled, landowning family, it was one whose fortunes had diminished with the war, when one of the main sources of revenue, letting grouse moors to rich Americans, had come to an end abruptly. In any case, it had always been understood and accepted by Angus that his elder brother, Lord Ogilvy, would inherit everything, and that he himself would earn his living. When Angus came to London at the age of twenty-three, he was given an allowance that was very small indeed, barely sufficient to cover his rent. The allowance lasted for only three years, during which time he was given the chance to prove himself in the City.

To supplement his income, Angus took various jobs, including a spell at the Savoy Hotel as a waiter. He quite enjoyed it until as a friend described 'he inadvertently dropped an omelette at the feet of an important diner, and his career came to an end'. Although money was always scarce, Angus managed to enjoy himself, as nearly all his friends of the same age were equally impoverished. They would often go to a certain nightclub where a mutually funded bottle of gin was kept for them, and brought out on each visit. Friendly waiters would tactfully conceal the prices of the wine and food from any girlfriend of the day, and although life was not easy, at least it was fun.

It was good luck combined with sure judgement that had given Ogilvy his first real break. A conversation he had with the economist Sir Roy Harrod during a weekend house party was overheard by Colonel Robert Adeane, a director of the Drayton Group of investment trusts. Adeane was impressed by what he overheard, and offered Angus a job at a modest salary, which he accepted. In fact circumstances had conspired to favour Angus – most of the facts he had quoted fresh from a chance reading of the *Financial Times* on the way to the house party. Still, what he had to say was more than mere repetition, and Adeane was quick to notice the young man's business acumen. As it turned out, his faith was well justified, and Ogilvy became a well-respected businessman.

For the few objectors who complained that it was quite unsuitable for a princess to marry a businessman, there was enough evidence to show that the Ogilvy family had played a romantic, if not all-important, part in British history. The warlike Ogilvy Scottish clan had played an important part in the English Civil War, supporting Charles I, and later in the Jacobite rebellion of 1745, and their women as well as their men had become renowned for courage and cunning, on more than one occasion excaping from prison in a quickly-donned disguise. The family seat was Airlie Castle, near Kirriemuir, Angus, and it was there that Alexandra took Marina just before Christmas 1962.

The Ogilvys were very much typical Scottish aristocracy at its best. Completely unsnobbish, and looked after by devoted estate workers, the atmosphere could not have been more welcoming for Alexandra and her mother. The newly engaged couple attended a ball for the estate workers given at the nearby Cortachy Castle, which Angus's brother, Lord Ogilvy, had lent for the occasion. The Earl's own Airlie Castle was too small for the dance; in 1956, extensive alteration to the building had been essential, for it was in danger of collapse, and consequently, it had been reduced in size to offer a more practical family home than the large, crumbling castle it had been.

Alexandra met many of the family retainers, including the nanny who had looked after Angus as a small boy, a very strong-willed old lady who was first rather guarded on meeting the Princess. But when Alexandra called to see the old lady, the Princess insisted on setting the table for afternoon tea and making it herself. Any doubts the nanny had were at once dispelled, as a result of Alexandra's thoughtfulness. 'This is the lassie for my Angus,' she remarked contentedly.

The weekend passed happily and Alexandra was shown the fascinating rooms at Cortachy, which had its full quota of ghosts, as would befit a Scottish castle.

One story ran that during the sixteenth-century, when the Ogilvys were under siege by the Campbells, a Campbell drummer boy was captured and, after giving false information, was thrown to his death over the Cortachy ramparts. Since then, the ghostly beating of his drum has often been reported when a member of the Airlie was about to die. Alexandra was taken to the room that the drummer was interrogated in, and was at once aware of the eerie atmosphere there. She later told a friend in London that she had to leave the room at once, for 'it was distinctly spooky, and I was terrified'.

Princess Mary, Alexandra's aunt, had also had a similar experience in the garden and was so shaken by what she felt, that she refused to talk about it for several days.

There were other disconcerting incidents. When Alexandra and Angus went out for a drive in the local countryside, the car skidded, turned over and was damaged, and they were both shaken and slightly bruised. Although Angus was sometimes accident prone, he could not be blamed for his car skidding in the treacherous icy roads. The couple decided to struggle home and say nothing, nevertheless. They were afraid that if Marina heard about it, she would insist that they should travel chauffeur driven in the future.

The discussion of the wedding plans, which began in Scotland that weekend, was continued in London after Alexandra and Angus returned there. Although the wedding would not be a state occasion, it would be a grand ceremonial occasion, and there was a great deal of careful planning to be organized for the actual day, which had now been chosen as Wednesday, 24 April 1963.

The best kept secret and the most carefully considered element was, of course, the bride's dress. Once again Cavanagh, who had scored such a striking success with the Duchess of Kent's dress, was asked to create a new design for Alexandra. He arrived at Kensington Palace early on for talks with Alexandra and Marina and heard that the young Princess had definite ideas for what she wanted. It had to be in lace, she said, with a simple classical design – above all, the dress was to have no frills or flounces.

Cavanagh even returned to his salon with two pieces of old lace, which Alexandra had studied. The first was a piece of Valenciennes lace which had belonged to Princess Marina's mother, and the other was a veil which had been last worn at the wedding of Princess Patricia of Connaught to the Hon. Alexander Ramsay. This piece, which had belonged to Queen Charlotte, wife of George III, was unsuitable for wearing in the 1960s, but that was not the point. Alexandra liked the pattern of tiny acorns and oak leaves worked in the design, and hoped that it could be copied in her own gown.

It was a challenge for Cavanagh, and one which gave him a few headaches. No weaver could be found to perform the task in England, so the old lace had to be sent to France, where a small company repeated the design in eighty yards of magnolia-tinted lace. Secrecy was carefully observed; a special arrangement was made with the

Customs to avoid declaring the large parcel when the completed work was sent to London. When the dress was nearly finished, Cavanagh had a brain-wave during one of the fittings. He felt that the twenty-one foot train could be worn as a veil, something which Alexandra thought was impossible. When the designer swept the cloth up, and draped it over her head, Alexandra was excited, and agreed that it was an inspiration. Marina's own lace was combined with the head-dress, and the whole piece was secured by a diamond tiara, which itself had been a wedding present to Marina from the City of London in 1934.

In the meantime, Angus was continuing with his job in the City, in as quiet a manner as possible. But it was impossible to avoid public scrutiny, and he was learning what it was like to be pursued by the press.

At that time, Angus lived in a small house in Culross Street in Mayfair.

A typical working day began with Angus rising at 5.30. His servant collected the car, after Angus had already seen business colleagues before nine o'clock, and drove him to a business meeting. Then at his office in the City, he would stay for lunch. He had often told his friends that he was too fond of wine to resist it, so he drank coffee instead. Later in the afternoon, after a brief shopping trip in the West End, he was back in the office, working until 8 p.m.

This typical day, would only leave Angus with a few hours' sleep, but he was so accustomed to his daily routine that he could not think of life in the City being any different when he married.

That of course had been agreed on, but there was the more difficult matter of a title to settle. The press assumed that Angus was offered a title and consequently refused, but this was only a guess, and the information has never been confirmed. In fact, it is likely that Angus was advised to accept a title for himself, in order at least to avoid the problem than any children of the marriage should be simply plain 'Mr' or 'Miss'. Anthony Armstrong-Jones had, it seemed, only reluctantly accepted his Earldom on marrying Princess Margaret, and by doing so had created a precedent which would have helped Angus. But, as a friend has said, Angus, for all his regard for tradition, felt strongly that title and honour had to be earned, and did not feel it would be fair to be given a peerage simply because he was marrying a princess. Barring any catastrophe, it was unlikely that any children would ever succeed to the throne, and so there was no absolute necessity for them to have a title.

The conservative *Evening Standard* was against a title for Angus. 'So far,' the columnist wrote, 'Mr Ogilvy appears to the peasant of this country as a sensible chap, with no lah-de-dah, and public opinion (we hope) still counts. What do the Palace panel want to call Mr Angus Ogilvy? Lord Ben Nevis? Count Killiecrankie?' The mocking reference to the Scottish mountain and a famous pass was an unkind stab at Lord Snowdon, whose title was taken from the mountain in Wales.

There were details of court etiquette other than titles which Angus would have to become used to. He would never be able to call the Queen, or Queen Elizabeth the Queen Mother, by their Christian names, for instance – they would always be 'Ma'm' to him. Strictly speaking, it was also the correct manner for Angus to address Princess Marina, but it was a formality which was relaxed for close friends in the Kent household. Outside their home, formality would undoubtedly make new demands. Like the Duke of Edinburgh and Lord Snowdon, Angus would never be able to walk alongside his wife in public, but instead would have to remain a few paces behind, and even his own friends and relatives would have to curtsy when they were presented to Alexandra.

The wedding plans unfolded, and the invitations were sent out. None of the refusals that had dogged Princess Margaret's wedding spoilt the arrangements. The Lord Chamberlain, who was responsible for the detailed programme, released the details in advance, and it was clear the wedding would be a colourful and exciting pageant, even if it was not to be a state ceremony. The programme was scheduled to the last minute:

10.30 The Queen and Prince Philip will leave Windsor Castle for Buckingham Palace accompanied by the Prince of Wales.

11.15 The non-royal guests will arrive at the entrance to Westminster Abbey.

11.15 The Bridegroom, with best man, will leave 10 Culross Street and arrive at the Cloister's Entrance in the Dean's Yard at 11.30.

11.20 The Bridesmaids and pages will leave Buckingham Palace in a motor-car procession and arrive at the Abbey's West Door at 11.30.

11.25 All foreign royal guests will leave Buckingham Palace in a motor car procession and arrive at the Abbey's West Door at 11.30.

11.30 Princess Marina, accompanied by the Duchess of Kent and Prince Michael, will leave Buckingham Palace by car, and arrive at the West Door of the Abbey at 11.45.

11.37 Royal guests with Princess Margaret, the Earl of Snowdon, the

Duke and Duchess of Gloucester, Prince William, Prince Richard, the Princess Royal, Princess Alice, Countess of Athlone, Princess Margarethe of Sweden and Princess Desiree of Sweden will be joined by the Queen Mother, who heads the procession as it passes Stable Yard Road junction with The Mall.

11.38 The procession will arrive at the Abbey's West Door.

11.43 The Duke of Kent with the bride, will leave Kensington Palace for the Abbey by car.

11.50 The Queen and Prince Philip accompanied by the Prince of Wales will arrive at the Abbey's West Door.

That was the official side of the wedding, but the many other preparations that had to be made included the wedding cake, which had already been begun by Lyons Caterers five weeks before the wedding itself, and was to be of truly royal stature. Standing five feet high and weighing one hundred and thirty pounds, it was made of three ten-sided tiers decorated with lattice work in icing. Alexandra had already sent the cake-makers a copy of her monogram, the intertwined double 'A's', which seemed so appropriate now. As an afterthought and a tribute to Angus, Alexandra also suggested the inclusion of five sets of miniature bagpipes, with the windbag in the colours of the Ogilvy tartan. The top tier was decorated with Alexandra roses, the middle with roses and thistles, and the bottom tier displayed Alexandra's and Angus's coat of arms.

The cake looked magnificent, especially as it was topped by a china vase supported by cupids and filled with Singapore orchids. The ingredients of the cake were equally impressive: 6 lb. butter, 6 lb. sugar, 70 eggs, $12\frac{1}{2}$ lb. currants, 7 lb. flour, 46 lb. marzipan, 25 lb. royal icing, spices, and not forgetting two bottles of rum and two of brandy.

Like any other bride, Alexandra was anxious to avoid duplication of her wedding presents, and it was she who was the first ever bride in the royal family to suggest a 'wants list', which she left with Harrods, the London department store. But even then the list was not drawn up in the common fashion. Harrods showed Alexandra some suitable items, with the prices concealed, and compiled a list from her choices.

Prospective givers simply ticked off what they wished to select for the couple, and as gifts arrived from elsewhere, Harrods were kept informed, and revised their list.

It was unlikely that Angus would choose a baby crocodile, as one groom had for his wife, as a Harrod's member of staff remarked, but if he did arrangements could later be made for it to be sent to the zoo.

Not all the gifts were items one could buy in a department store, however. Alexandra's church in Kensington sent a gold Spode dinner service; the Grand Lodge of English freemasons an antique pair of French Candelabra; and the Council and Staff of the Guide Dog for the Blind Association gave four George III pierced salt cellars.

On the groom's side, the people of the County of Angus chose a Chippendale writing desk, and the local tradespeople a silver coffee-pot. The tenants of Airlie and Cortachy, who had made Alexandra so welcome, commissioned pictures of various local scenes. Everywhere the flow of presents reflected the high regard in which Alexandra was held, but perhaps the most touching was a gilt mirror, subscribed to by the Royal Commonwealth Society for the Blind, of which Alexandra is the President.

As Kensington Palace, in liaison with the Lord Chamberlain's office worked overtime to finalize the details, Alexandra herself was at last able to slip out to Bond Street, to make a few last-minute purchases. At the same time, all over Europe, the royal families who were sending representatives, were finishing their packing.

They had been invited by the Queen and Duke of Edinburgh to a ball in honour of Alexandra and Angus, which was to be held in Windsor Castle. The guest list of nearly two thousand was to make it one of the grandest occasions Windsor had seen for many years, and was in fact one of the last great celebrations of its kind. The great Waterloo Chamber was decked out with thousands of flowers and over eight hundred pot plants, brought from the royal nurseries.

Over a hundred guests dined with the Queen, the Kents, and other members of the Ogilvy family, and the preparations must have reminded the older staff of the great days of the past. The food ordered included 80 lb. of smoked salmon, 500 ounces of caviar, 200 chickens, 50 ducks, 36 turkeys, 2 barons of beef, 14 large legs of pork, and 24 hams. The mammoth banquet was prepared by a hundred and forty staff, and a hundred and twenty extra hands had been hired to help with the washing-up. Drinks for guests at the ball included 1,600 bottles of champagne, 15 dozen cases of whisky, 10 cases of gin, 3 cases of vodka, and 2,000 bottles of lager. The total cost of the evening was estimated at between £15,000 and £20,000, but it did not come from public money, as it was the personal gift of the Queen to Alexandra and

Angus, and a tribute from somebody who knew as well as anyone just what a priceless asset Alexandra was to the country.

Nevertheless, a sour note was struck by the *Daily Express*, which particularly jibed at the collection of exiled monarchs who had been invited to the Ball:

What's going on? Is this a marriage between two popular young people, or is it a . . . campaign for Europe's busted down pensioned off purpled off, forgotten but not buried, Royals from Spain, Austria and Italy? Why should the Alex and Angus romance degenerate into a rollicking group for Royal exiles, pretenders and pensioners? Is this the Welfare state or the Royal Welfare Morgue? Ex King Umberto of Italy (pause for chuckles) is billed at this royal performance, but you can bet that he won't be footing the bill. He started his reign in 1946, and had to pack it in after a month.

How many bottles of Gran Marc (non-vintage champagne) is this cove Umberto entitled to?

Ex Queen Eugenie of Spain . . . is here in London, for the do, kissed on her gloved hand by Princess Marina at London airport, and then on both cheeks. Hell, the Spanish monarch fell in 1931, five years before Princess Alexandra was born. Here's another cough drop. Archduke Ferdinand of Austria. The Austrian monarchy sank without a trace in 1918. Anyway, half of these are the names used to frighten us when we were nippers in the First World War. . . .

The paper even went on to attack the Count of Paris, who had shown Alexandra such hospitality when she was attending her finishing school in Paris. Although the criticism was harsh, there was perhaps a measure of truth in the accusation that it seemed out of touch with popular feeling to invite so many royal figures from abroad, many of whom even had no recognition in their own country. But then it was not a state wedding, and the ball was designed to please the young couple, even if the choice of guests was more Marina's than theirs. And if Angus regarded the whole affair as a slightly terrifying prospect, there is no doubt that for him and Alexandra the evening was one of the most memorable of their lives.

The evening had begun eventfully. After a private rehearsal with Alexandra at Westminster Abbey, Angus had gone back to Culross Street to change for the ball, and then drove to Windsor via Kensington Palace. As he drove towards Albert Hall, a station-wagon braked suddenly at a zebra crossing, and although only doing three miles an hour Angus crashed into the back of the vehicle with his Jaguar. He suffered a cut on his head, but after the police were called in, he was able to continue his journey in his dented car.

At nine o'clock, after the dinner, the Queen entered the ballroom with Prince Philip, and as they did so Joe Loss and his band struck up a Strauss waltz. At a signal from the Queen, the first dance was led by Alexandra and Angus and everybody remarked on how beautiful the Princess looked in her long close-fitting gown of snow-white silk. Her hair was gathered up and crowned with a tiara which Angus had given her, which she wore for the first time. The white platinum mount shimmered with flower petals set with diamond, and centred with pearls. The practical Scot had also arranged that the pearls could be unscrewed and replaced with turquoises for less formal occasions.

After the gracious opening, the ball swung into a glittering, celebratory mood, and the dancing began. Any thought that it was an event staged mainly for elderly monarchs could be dismissed after midnight, when the waltzes and foxtrots that had characterized the early evening's entertainment changed to the twist, the youthful and uninhibited fashion at the time. Even the Queen and the Duke of Edinburgh laughingly took part.

No doubt itching to join in this part of the festivities were Prince Charles and Princess Anne, who were too young to attend the ball, but were allowed to sit in a gallery overlooking the magnificent scene, which they filmed with a ciné camera.

As the night progressed, heat from the lights caused the plants and flowers to wilt. They were discreetly revived by the royal gardeners with small watering cans, but any of the guests who felt the same discomfort as the plants managed to disguise it. Many stayed at the ball until three o'clock, and crowds waited near the Castle to watch them depart. Princess Margaret and Lord Snowdon were cheered loudly as they left for Kensington in the early dawn light.

Alexandra spent the following day, the last before her wedding, quietly in Kensington Palace. She had been amongst the last of the guests to leave, and spent the morning recuperating. In the afternoon, Princess Anne, who was to be chief bridesmaid, arrived for afternoon tea, to discuss with Alexandra the last details. The Queen provided several luxury coaches for the party, into which the royals piled. They lunched at a public house in Bray, and the whole day was an experience which must have been quite unusual for the visitors, and certainly a total contrast with the pomp of the following day.

Angus was proving to be a lively and entertaining host. In the evening, he dined with his own family in Claridges, and as he dropped in to see Alexandra on the way there he was a little late in arriving at the hotel. He was in a relaxed mood, however, and soon turned the evening into something of a party, happily playing a game of musical chairs with his guests in their private room, while deftly balancing coffee and liqueurs on a tray.

His party broke up at 10.45, and after taking his parents to St James's Palace, where they were staying for the night, he drove to his own house in Mayfair. He had been followed by the press the moment he left Claridges, and when he finally got out of his car he astonished the photographers and reporters who arrived with him by remarking, 'This has been quite a day. Come in and have a drink with me. You deserve it. Er . . . strictly off the record of course.'

Angus was learning to show the press the same consideration that had made Alexandra so popular with them. Later, he would usually tell the press exactly where he was taking Alexandra. On the occasions when he wanted privacy he had only to say, 'But we want to be quite alone tonight', and his wishes were nearly always respected.

That night, London had something of a festival atmosphere. Someone noticed Alexandra glancing out of a window in Kensington Palace before drawing the curtains, and the huge crowds that had been gathering from the early evening erupted into cheers. In the Mall, thousands had arrived in blankets, mattresses and camping equipment, waiting for the departures and arrivals the next day. Many had arrived in the hope of finding a good viewing spot, but the police had given instructions that no camping would be allowed before midnight. The crowds flowed instead into St James's Park, and started an impromptu celebration. Hot dog stalls and ice-cream vendors, plus beer from local pubs near Victoria, helped to create a party atmosphere, and those who were not too tired, danced to the music from transistor radios.

Many small children were tucked into sleeping bags, completely undisturbed by the sound of merry making. One girl who managed to find a place under the shelter of the trees in the Mall said, 'I am South African, but in my heart I always will be English.'

As Londoners prepared for the wedding, full of anticipation for the couple and their happiness, the weather forecast seemed unfavourable. That did not seem to matter, however, for even if it poured, nothing would spoil the enjoyment of those who wanted to contribute to the pleasure of the Princess who to so many was simply 'Alexandra the Greatest'.

# 14

# *Mrs Ogilvy*

WHILE MARINA, ALONG with everyone else at Kensington Palace, was feeling extremely nervous on the morning of the wedding, the chief performer, Alexandra, was said to be the least anxious. Even so, she was unable to eat breakfast, but she was composed enough to advise those around her that they must all keep calm.

Alexandra had risen early, and welcomed her hairdresser and John Cavanagh, who was to check that the wedding dress fitted as perfectly as he had planned. Prince Edward, who was to give Alexandra away, had flown in from Hong Kong, where his regiment was stationed.

At last everything seemed to be organized, and the young Duke waited for his sister to appear. No one expected Alexandra to be ready on time. Perhaps as Angus was dressing in Mayfair, he recalled an occasion when he had arranged to meet Alexandra at the theatre. Angus waited for her for over twenty minutes, when he suddenly realized that he had arrived at the wrong place. Hurriedly taking a taxi to the right theatre, and expecting a mild rebuke, he looked up when he arrived, and saw no sign of the Princess. A moment or so later another taxi appeared, and out stepped Alexandra, apologizing profusely for keeping her fiancé waiting. But on her wedding day she surprised everyone, including herself, by being ready punctually. She drove off with her brother in the open Rolls-Royce, which was the Queen's own personal car, and was followed by Marina in her dark blue Rolls, with its distinctive registration plate YR II.

By now, the first guests had arrived at the Abbey, and it was a superb array of high ceremonial fashion. Princess Margaret was smiling and happy in a silk coat embroidered with primroses and a lemon-coloured toque. The young Duchess of Kent, with Hong Kong not far from her mind, was distinguished by her delicate coral pink matching dress and coat, with a 'coolie' style hat. Finally all eyes turned onto the bride's mother.

Marina could always be counted on to look magnificent, and today was no exception. Her dress of gold tissue was covered with tiny gold spangles, and her enormous matching gold hat, apparently based on a cavalier head-dress with its sloping upturned brim, gloriously crowned the outfit.

Queen Elizabeth the Queen Mother was one of the last of the British royal guests to arrive, in a coat and dress of silver lace on a bluebell tulle. Her hat of osprey feathers waved in the slight breeze as she was welcomed into the Abbey. Then a fanfare of trumpets heralded the arrival of the Queen, in pale green silk organza. So delicately embroidered was the Queen's hat, with minute lily-of-the-valley, that they seemed to float in the air as she walked down the nave with the Duke of Edinburgh and Prince Charles.

The bridal attendants were waiting at the West Door for Alexandra's arrival. Their dresses were made of heavy magnolia silk serge, weighty enough to keep the shape of the bell sleeves, a feature of John Cavanagh's spring collection. Cavanagh had thoughtfully kept the bridesmaid's outfits off the floor to avoid their tripping for, with the exception of Princess Anne, they were all very young. As it was, the twelve-year-old Princess Anne, who looked very mature with her hair swept up for the first time, had the difficult task of keeping the little girls in order. Once or twice she had to whisper in French to the tiny Elizabeth Arch-Duchess of Austria, who was as mischievous as any girl of six. The two page boys were David Ogilvy, Angus's nephew, and Marina's private secretary's son, Simon Hay.

When Alexandra herself appeared, the full beauty of her dress was apparent. Small gold sequins were undersewn in the gown and it shimmered under the light of the television cameras. There were strict instructions that the couple's faces were not to be filmed until they were actually man and wife, but behind the scenes, informal photographs were allowed, and Marina and Princess Anne were seen arranging Alexandra's train.

Alexandra was used to the glare of the public eye, and although nervous, managed to keep smiling. Angus, on the other hand, was less used to such exposure, and his groom, Peregrine Fairfax, an old school friend, had to make a few jokes to keep him cheerful.

Alexandra, lightly grasping her brother's arm, looked relaxed and confident as she walked down the long aisle towards the altar. In the historic Abbey, with the various different coloured outfits contributing to the splendour, it was an impressive scene, and one which paid indirect homage to Queen Victoria, with so many of her European descendants under the one roof.

Among them was Queen Eugenie of Spain, one of her great grand-daughters, for whom it must have been a particularly moving occasion. As a bride, a terrorist had thrown a bomb at her, killing sixty people in the watching crowd. Queen Eugenie's coach was thrown on its side, and although she was unhurt, her dress and shoes were splattered with blood. Memories of that day must have returned to the old lady as she watched the peaceful scene.

There were in contrast many quite ordinary people there, rubbing shoulders with royalty in a way totally apt for the popular, informal Alexandra. Angus had not forgotten his char lady from Culross Street, nor the Airlie and Cortachy estate workers, whose coach and hotel expenses he had met, so that they could be present. Alexandra had also remembered those who looked after her, and had made seats available for people like the assistant from the Marks and Spencer store, near Marble Arch, which she used so much.

The colour came not only from the wedding guests, but from the huge urns overflowing with cherry blossom, roses, hyacinths and rhododendrons. As Alexandra and Angus reached the altar, the music of the hymn 'Holy, Holy, Holy, Lord God Almighty' heralded a moment of fright noticed by Marina. Angus had to be restrained from walking too quickly, because the veil attached to the head-dress was dragging on the pile of the thick carpet threatening to pull off the whole veil and tiara. The tiara wobbled uncertainly, until Alexandra took a firm grasp on Angus's arm and Marina was able to sit back with a sigh of relief.

The religious ceremony followed the traditional lines of the Book of Common Prayer, with the young bride promising to 'obey' despite the fact that the Ogilvy family were Christian Scientists, and Angus himself had been a member until comparatively recently before his wedding. The service was conducted by Dr Ramsay, the Archbishop of Canterbury, and the Rev H. L. O. Tees, from St Mary Abbots, the Kents' own church in Kensington. There was no sermon, but in its place the vicar read a lesson from St Paul's Epistle to the Corinthians.

After the wedding hymn, 'Love Divine, all loves excelling' the Princess and Angus went through to the Chapel of St Edward the Confessor to sign the marriage registers. After they had been witnessed by the Queen and other members of the royal family, Alexandra turned to the young Princess Anne, and remarked, 'Your turn next?' to which the twelve-year-old Princess could only reply, 'Me?'

At last to the strains of Widor's toccata, Princess Alexandra, now the Hon. Mrs Angus Ogilvy, made her way with her husband to the Abbey door.

All was well, for the page boys had remembered their instructions not to tread on the train, and the west door was safely reached. Instead of the Rolls-Royce in which Alexandra had arrived, the Queen had requested that the famous Glass Coach, drawn by four grey horses, should take the newly married couple to St James's Palace for the wedding breakfast.

The waiting crowds, who had seen none of the ceremony, were in ebullient mood when their long vigil was rewarded. Escorted by some of the Household Cavalry, Alexandra and Angus were seen for the first time as man and wife. Along the lengths of the processional route, from Parliament Square to Parliament Street, down Whitehall, through Horse Guards Arch, and finally into the Mall, the couple were greeted with shouts of 'Good old Alex!', and 'Well done, Angus!'

When the coach finally entered St James's Palace by the Garden Gate, the Ogilvys were ready to welcome over seventy guests for the breakfast. But first, they went up to the throne-room with other members of the family for photographs. Princess Margaret, happily smoking a cigarette, directed the attendants as they arranged Alexandra's dress and train.

At last, an hour later, the celebrations reached their climax when Angus and Alexandra climbed the small dais to the picture gallery, and cut the first slice of the cake. After it was done, Angus brandished the knife and, at last able to relax after the morning's ordeal, called to his wife, 'Go on, now you do the rest.'

After the formality of the ceremony itself, this reception was a welcoming and enjoyable one. Lady Moyra Hamilton carried Alexandra's train as the Princess chatted to the various guests. Then she slipped over to Clarence House, to change into a bright flamingo-pink wool suit, with a cream silk blouse, and matching turban hat. Angus also changed into a less formal suit, and together they were ready to leave for Heathrow from Friary Court, in Marina's car. They were given a traditional enthusiastic send-off. Prince Charles and Prince Juan Carlos threw rice and confetti at the couple, and the over-eager

Queen even stepped on to the King of Norway's toes in her anxiety to have a good view.

The first stage of the honeymoon was to be spent at Birkhall in Deeside, the Scottish home of Queen Elizabeth the Queen Mother, and after a week there they were to fly out to Marbella in Spain.

At Heathrow, the Ogilvys stopped for a moment to receive a representative of the press, and Alexandra told him, 'Now the ordeal's over, we do want to thank everyone for being so kind.'

But the ordeal was not quite finished. The plane had to be diverted from Aberdeen to Lossiemouth due to the heavy fog. The station commander of the R.A.F. base at Lossiemouth was about to give a dinner party, and was astonished to find the Ogilvys at his door, requesting shelter until alternative arrangements were made for their travel on to Birkhall.

The last thing anybody could have expected on the day of the royal wedding was to have the couple knock on their door, but the R.A.F. coped admirably. Over drinks and sandwiches, the Ogilvys watched an edited version of their wedding on the television of the station commander, Kirke, Alexandra finding it so exciting that she could hardly bear to watch it. When she finally left with her husband for the 85 mile drive to Birkhall, crowds had already heard of the Ogilvys' arrival at Lossiemouth, and waited to cheer them on their way.

Tired but happy, they eventually reached Birkhall just before midnight, ready to relax away from the eye of publicity, and to plan their new home, Thatched House Lodge in Richmond Park.

It had been a memorable day. Life now would be very different for Angus, not only because of the public role his wife had to play. Once he had joked, 'I am too old for marriage. No girl can catch me.' Settling down with a wife would no doubt keep him busy, but although hardly old, Angus had a maturity at thirty-four which helped him to be positive about the direction of his own life. Alexandra would come to appreciate his wisdom and down-to-earth approach to matters, and perhaps above all the lack of pretension which matched her own nature.

The period of the engagement was not easy for either of them. The Princess at least had the protection of the household of Kensington Palace. But Angus was in a very much more exposed position. He said at the time that he would not have survived but for one very remarkable woman whom he described as 'the best secretary in the world'. She had been with him since 1951: Joan Neale.

# 15

# *Together*

THE PRIVACY THAT the Ogilvys hoped for was on the whole respected by the press. Angus and Alexandra wanted to enjoy their honeymoon in complete quiet, and they only emerged from Birkhall to attend morning service at Crathie Parish Church, where the royal family worshipped when they were staying at Balmoral. They drove there in an old pre-war shooting brake that belonged to Queen Elizabeth the Queen Mother.

Spotting the waiting cameras, the couple ignored tradition, and instead of entering the church by the side door normally used by the royal family, they entered by the main door and paused for a moment to allow the press some photographs. They had greeted the reporters with a cheerful 'Good morning', and the cameras captured the Princess in her turquoise hat.

Amongst the photographers that morning was one destined to cause trouble, Ray Bellisario. He was already well known to the royal family, having often taken 'candid' shots of them, which caused quite a furore when they appeared in the newspapers. Bellisario was a freelance operator, and regarded the Queen and her relations as fair game. He would go to great lengths to obtain shots of his subjects in circumstances which the royal family considered to be private. He had even received a police warning to desist from bothering Princess Margaret, and the Queen had at one point issued a complaint about the photographer through her press office.

He was also well known to Alexandra, who adopted a practical approach and managed to avoid problems with him by always giving him her co-operation. It was easier for her to agree to a photograph than to refuse, she agreed, and for once Bellisario was satisfied and departed.

She had learned this when once in Florence with Marina. The photographer followed them around until, on their third day there,

Marina complained that he was being a nuisance. She politely asked him to leave, but Alexandra asked the man what he wanted. Bellisario explained that what he wanted was, simply, a pose of the Princess at a table sipping a soft drink, and although Marina continued to object, Alexandra agreed. The photograph was taken, and Bellisario left.

Although Angus became familiar with the photographer by sight, he never actually met him, although he had been included amongst the press men that Angus invited to his home for drinks the night before he was married.

That evening was the cause of the problems on the honeymoon. Bellisario claims that Angus promised him and the other pressmen interested that they would be allowed to take photographs of him and Alexandra on their honeymoon, and that when this was not forthcoming he decided to take what shots he could get. Bellisario has insisted that he felt betrayed by Angus going back on his word, for when he tried to see Angus at Crathie, both he and the Princess refused him his request to take photographs. In fact, other reports suggest that the conversation Bellisario alleges he had with Angus never took place, and Angus certainly never knowingly met him.

Whatever the facts, Bellisario felt that he could go to whatever lengths were required to get honeymoon photographs. His first attempt was a failure. The Aberdeenshire police had been warned to keep press away from the road that circled around the Birkhall estate, and when Bellissario tried to take up a position overlooking the house, he was asked to leave by an inspector.

After an argument, the policeman left, and the following morning Bellisario returned, having parked his car in Ballater so that the police would think he was there. An obliging friend dropped him off at a secluded spot near the River Muick, three quarters of a mile from Birkhall.

After a wait of several hours, his patience was rewarded when Angus and Alexandra appeared, and settled down to enjoy a picnic. The photographer could just make out through his telescopic lens their figures, and their groundsheet and hamper. The couple had chosen a spot near the river, unseen by anyone but Bellisario.

Any pictures he could make out were not in close detail as far as he could see, but he focused his extra-long telescopic lens on Alexandra and Angus and hoped for the best.

Rain soon drove the couple indoors, but when they came out again

Bellisario continued with his illicit photographs. When he had finished, he sent them ahead of himself to London to be processed. Once in London he was told that sales were good, especially to foreign magazines, and when he saw the results, Bellisario realized why. The results were better than he had imagined. Unwittingly he had taken what he described as 'a love story in pictures'. Eventually, he decided that it was impossible to print the series, although he did sell some of Alexandra picking a four-leaf clover.

Alexandra and Angus were naturally furious when they learned of the photographs, and the only consolation was that Bellisario promised them that he would never publish them, although he refused to destroy the negatives. It was a harsh introduction to public life for Angus.

The rest of the Scottish part of their honeymoon was peaceful, and Alexandra did everything possible to enact her desire for as little fuss as possible. Alexandra had once remarked that she found 'luxury faintly stifling.' Staff were temporarily reduced at Birkhall, until the royal couple were attended by only eight servants. Two of Alexandra's maids and two footmen came from Kensington Palace, and the other four were part-time helpers recruited from Ballater.

After the week at Birkhall, the couple flew to spend a month on the estate of the Duke of Alba at Marbella, only to encounter the same problem there. They lived in the Duke's summer house, and passed many hours strolling in the sun, although at first Alexandra was afraid to go out, being wary of snooping photographers. She was convinced that a cameraman was hidden in a tree overlooking the house, which was unfortunately near the public road. In fact, she was correct, but on being discovered the man refused to move. The Spanish police had to be called in, and obligingly started to cut the tree down, but the photographer would not leave, and told Angus that unless he got the shots he required he would lose his job. Angus very kindly told the man that he and Alexandra would shop in the village the following day at a certain time. While they would not pose, the man could take his photographs, provided that he would then leave them in peace.

This went according to plan, but at once a rival newspaper photographer insisted on having the same consideration as the other. This was granted, but the first paper then gained publicity by publishing a leader with the photographs saying that Angus had asked them to take it. Press attention was beginning to turn into a nightmare, but Alexandra and Angus did not antagonize the photographers and did succeed in finding a modicum of privacy.

While Angus and Alexandra were still in Spain, work began to make their new home habitable. They had spent a week looking for somewhere suitable, and decided that to begin their married life they would rent Thatched House Lodge in Richmond Park from the Duchess of Sutherland, for an initial period of five years.

The house, standing in a large acreage of the royal park, offered seclusion without a feeling of being locked in, and had six bedrooms, five reception rooms, a drawing-room and kitchen quarters. Later, changes were made to accommodate offices and then a nursery. There was also a heated swimming pool, a stable block and several cottages which would house domestic staff.

It was not a particularly large house, indeed by royal standards it was extremely small. Thatched House Lodge had been built for the then Prime Minister, Sir Robert Walpole, and in more recent years, had been the war office of the American High Command. General Eisenhower had taken a small suite of rooms there, and enjoyed visits to the old gazebo in the garden, which had rooms decorated by Angelica Kauffmann, or possibly by her husband Zucchi, in the fashionable rococo style.

Angus and Alexandra moved into their new home after their honeymoon and Angus eventually sold his batchelor flat in Culross Street in Mayfair to a Californian businessman. The upkeep of Thatched House Lodge was expensive, and the initial rent of £2,000 absorbed nearly all of Angus's income. The various extra costs of decorating the house were mainly paid for by Angus, and so he must indeed have had to keep a careful eye on expenditure, not something usually associated with royal newly-weds. When Angus married he had resigned some of his directorships, and as the remainder were held on behalf of the Drayton Group rather than for himself, his income was not as large as was supposed.

Being neither the sister nor the daughter of the reigning monarch, Alexandra did not receive a fixed allowance on the Civil List, although she could claim back a contribution towards expenses incurred on official duties including staff salaries. The wedding presents were perhaps more welcome and necessary than those given to other members of the royal family.

Angus had a natural gift for design and colour. He had cherished at one time the notion to be an architect, and had never lost his interest in the subject. In view of this, Alexandra left to him much of the decoration of their new home. He added some bathrooms, new dressing-rooms, and made suggestions for antique furniture. He had also inherited his mother's impeccable taste, and before long, had transformed what some regarded as rather an ugly house into a comfortable and beautiful home.

The only inconvenience about Thatched House Lodge was its distance from London, which could be troublesome both for Angus travelling to the City and for Alexandra's engagements. He stuck to his City routine, although he reduced his working hours, generally leaving the office after the rush hour. Alexandra, at one time not an early riser and often not up before ten, now changed to getting up at seven o'clock, so that she could breakfast with Angus. They have continued their married life in the way they began; trying not to let their separate worlds dominate the other. Angus once remarked to a friend, 'I don't bore Alexandra with my daily routine, and she doesn't bore me with hers!'

At home the atmosphere is, as one friend has described it, that of a 'loving cosy couple'. They have friends whenever possible for dinner, but often their entertaining is return hospitality to some foreign visitor to this country, for they both do far more than is ever printed in the Court Circular.

Before long they were settled into a comfortable, friendly home, although Angus's insistence that he should carry on with his job as far as possible and only take part in royal functions when it was natural that Alexandra should be accompanied by her husband, caused a few difficulties at the start of their life together. Eyebrows were raised in the first year of their marriage when it was noted that Angus only attended Ascot for one day. A guest of the Queen at Windsor Castle, he travelled to work in the City as usual on the other days.

He received a mild ticking-off from the Queen, but he explained to her that earning his living was his duty and an absolute necessity, something the Queen came to understand and respect. From the point of view of the royal family, it was a novel and disconcerting situation that one of their ranks should be involved in another world, and in such an alien one as business, but through force of character and breadth of vision, which came partly from this varied life style. Angus soon allayed their anxieties.

On 28 July 1963 it was announced that, on medical advice, Princess Alexandra was undertaking no further engagements. It sounded like bad news to the uninitiated, but it was really quite the reverse. The phrase meant she was expecting a baby. Her last engagement was a visit to Durham, where Alexandra presented new colours to the 8th Battalion of the Durham Light Infantry, as their Colonel-in-Chief. Later, plans went ahead to adapt some rooms in Thatched House Lodge to make a nursery, and twice a week Alexandra attended pre-natal relaxation classes in natural childbirth.

During the months that followed, events prevented Alexandra from enjoying the stress-free relaxation she needed. A kitchen fire from a refrigerator could be laughed off, but not the lack of security which allowed a burglary to take place early in November, when Alexandra and Angus were there.

The Princess went up to her bedroom and surpised an intruder, who was going through her jewel box. She screamed loudly, and the burglar jumped out of the window through which he had entered and ran off into the grounds. Angus, who thought his wife had suffered a fall, rushed upstairs in alarm, and when he learned what had happened, called the police. A search was carried out, and it was discovered that the man had taken many of their wedding presents, including a gold cigarette case inscribed to Angus from the Queen and Prince Philip, a pearl and diamond tie-pin, and a gold watch set in a twenty-dollar gold piece which had been a gift from Alexandra to Angus. Most distinctive of all was a ruby and diamond brooch, a present from Princess Olga, Marina's sister.

The theft was bad enough, but more alarming was the effect of the shock suffered by Alexandra in her delicate state. She was concerned about being left alone, and worried particularly as Angus was due to leave for Spain for a weekend business trip. At the last moment, Alexandra decided to go with him, and they flew to Madrid tourist class.

While they were away, security was tightened up at Thatched House Lodge, but if this was a problem in England, it at least had a certain amusing side abroad. Massive protection was given to Alexandra by the Spanish Civil Guard, who kept the usual flock of reporters away from the Princess while she was in Spain.

While Angus was at a business meeting, Alexandra arranged to meet her cousin, Princess Sofia, in the private rooms of a bank. As Angus's meeting finished sooner than he expected, he decided to meet his wife and her cousin, and arrived at the bank. He asked if the English

Princess was there, and after a guard had spoken to a colleague, Angus was taken to a scantily furnished room and locked in. The police had decided that he was an English journalist.

Meanwhile, Alexandra was puzzled that her husband had not turned up, and began to ask questions about where he had gone. Officials explained that the only Englishman they had seen was a journalist, whom they were detaining until after the Princess had left. Alexandra who knew all the press who were covering the visit, asked for the offender's description. She quickly guessed that it was Angus, and he was released after Alexandra had formally identified him, much to police embarrassment.

The police in London had not been idle either, for when the couple returned home they heard that a man had been arrested for possessing a ruby suspected to belong to Alexandra. It turned out that this man, picked up through the offices of a police informant, had managed to dispose of the goods before his arrest, and the stones were unfortunately not recovered.

Alexandra was meanwhile more concerned with thoughts of her new baby, and when the royal family celebrated the New Year at Sandringham, it became clear that in the future another venue would have to be chosen for family celebrations, for not only was Alexandra expecting a baby, but so also were the Queen, the Duchess of Kent, and Princess Margaret. Windsor Castle would for a time be more capable of coping with the sudden increase in nannies and nursery maids.

While Alexandra was in the last months of her pregnancy, with no engagements to attend, she was free to shop and prepare for the event in a leisurely way, although this could be interrupted by the notorious sudden whims. Once, when in a hairdressing salon, she had a sudden passion for some fish and chips. An assistant was sent out to a fish restaurant, and although a plate and knife and fork were provided, Alexandra happily ate them from the newspaper wrappings.

It was a time to be with Angus, and when the couple decided to lunch in a small Marylebone restaurant, problems began. Angus left his wife in the car, while he enquired from the head waiter whether there was a free table. The man indicated that there were only two places available, but that they would have to share a table. As Angus left to collect Alexandra, the waiter suddenly recognized him, and persuaded other diners to move to another table.

When they returned, the Ogilvys enjoyed some pasta and a glass of red wine. The proprietor refused to accept payment, and unwilling to make a scene in the face of his insistence the Ogilvys reluctantly agreed. While they appreciated the generosity of the management, they were as keen as ever to follow the unwritten rule that the royal family always pay the same price as everyone else.

It was a happy time, and they enjoyed several outings, whenever possible going incognito in their constant wish to avoid formality and shun V.I.P. treatment. It was not always possible however.

During a visit to Hampton Court, they queued for coffee at a self-service stall, certain that no one would recognize them in their casual clothes. It was too much to hope for, and within a few minutes crowds had gathered to watch the Princess and her husband enjoying their snack. They were obliged to retreat to their car, and drive off.

At the best of times, the couple could only take risks when they felt that the coast was probably clear, but they could never be certain. It was a compromise, but Alexandra clearly did not intend to be driven into the pattern of only emerging from indoors with an entourage of protective servants. As her confinement approached, however, and public attention intensified, Alexandra became more restricted in her movements.

# 16

# *Happy Family*

ALEXANDRA'S BABY WAS expected on 16 February 1964, and as that date approached the Superintendent of the Middlesex Hospital moved into Thatched House Lodge. In fact, the baby chose a much later date to arrive, and one just as memorable as Alexandra's own birthday of Christmas Day.

Shortly after mid-day on 29 February, in the presence of Angus, a nine-pound boy was born. Everything went smoothly, and a message was sent to a delighted Queen at Buckingham Palace. Alexandra herself remarked, 'It was bad enough for me, sharing a birthday on Christmas Day. I didn't want my poor child only to have birthdays every four years!'

The baby was thirteenth in line to the throne, an unlucky position which was rectified when Prince Edward was born on 10 March. Nor was the jubilation just local. The baby's arrival was even celebrated in the Spanish town of Jerez, where a cask of sherry was dedicated to him, with fifty gallons reserved for his own use. Nearer home, in the Airlie estate in Scotland, the landlord of the Ogilvy Arms at Kirriemuir immediately announced free drinks for everyone. Another group of friends nearer home was the Women's Institute at Iver, of which Alexandra had remained a member throughout the years, and Alexandra was delighted to learn that she was being sent a premium bond on the child's behalf.

It was decided to call the new arrival James Robert Bruce, a choice which reflected Angus's family origins. Almost at once, a horoscope was cast:

He will take more after his mother than his father, though in later years it will be obvious that his father shared in his upbringing. He will be educated without a fuss, and later will take up a profession with a leaning towards draughtsmanship. He will be sensitive by nature, yet persistent too. His love for animals will be noticed from an early age, and his handling of them as he grows older will be much admired. . . . He will excel in horsemanship and painting. Music will attract him too, but to a lesser degree.

Both mother and son progressed admirably, and before James was christened, Alexandra made her first public appearance since his birth, at a 250th anniversary service at St Anne's Church, Kew Green, in Surrey. She was given a huge reception, for it was known that the baby was to be christened the following day, 11 May.

The christening photographs were taken, at Buckingham Palace, not by Lord Snowdon, who had just become a father himself, but by Cecil Beaton. James wore the traditional Honiton lace, but also a beautiful white robe, which had been worked by crippled women who were confined to a London Hospital. It was a gesture which indicated the widespread feelings of love and affection for Alexandra, as well as the importance Alexandra attached to them.

Despite the memories of being mobbed on several occasions by an over-enthusiastic public, Alexandra took the risk of walking with her baby in a pram in Richmond Park. As it turned out, she was never troubled by anyone as she braved the spring chill, and although recognized, was given the privacy she deserved.

The arrival of the baby meant a reduction of space in Thatched House Lodge, as one of the spare bedrooms became a nursery, and another was converted into a bed-sitting room for the new nanny, Miss Olive Rattle. Nurse Rattle was the ideal nanny, and soon fitted into the household. There was of course no shortage of toys or clothes, for many well-wishers, including many from Australia, sent cuddly bears, kangaroos, and assorted woollens. But perhaps one of the most beautiful gifts was a pillow-case with matching pram cover, embroidered with delicate snowdrops. Sent by a friend of the Ogilvys, it was made from silk taken from one of the few silk farms in England.

As the enlarged family settled down to their new life, Alexandra's public duties were reduced to give her time for James. Angus had wisely decided to stick to his plan of only accompanying Alexandra on certain occasions, but he may well have wondered in retrospect how his wife had managed to fulfil her engagements on her small allowance before they were married. By this time, Angus was having selflessly to divert large parts of his own income towards the expense of his wife's public life. With the hard work necessary to do this, and the additional demands of the considerable charity work he undertook, the pressure on him inevitably led to a deterioration of his health.

Despite this, he cancelled a holiday to Sardinia in 1964 because of pressing business commitments. It was a time of anxiety for other reasons too. Alexandra had been subjected to a series of anonymous letters written as it transpired, by a mental case. Fortunately, security was increased at Thatched House Lodge, and it was soon proved necessary when another man tried to gain access to the house by pretending to be a member of the royal family. Yet another nuisance was a woman who persistently tried to see Alexandra for no reason, and although she was quite harmless, it only increased the pressure on the family.

In mid-November, Alexandra was installed as the first Chancellor of the new University of Lancaster. The building had been constructed out of a converted furniture factory, and it was seen as an equally innovative venture in education. While Alexandra was there, Angus had been persuaded to to into St Mary's Hospital, as it was feared that he was suffering from nervous exhaustion. A week's rest was prescribed, and the Ogilvys decided to take a holiday at long last.

They had planned to take a ski-ing holiday in Switzerland, motoring across the Continent towards the Alps and following their previous practice of travelling under a false name, and staying at small hotels quite unrecognized.

But their first attempt failed. They were obliged to return to London in mid-January 1965, when they heard of the death of Sir Winston Churchill, and hurried back for the state funeral. Afterwards, they left again for Switzerland to continue their holiday, but Alexandra had to break it up by flying back briefly to launch a ship in Belfast. This hectic shuttle to and fro was the only way in which Alexandra could have some sort of relaxation and attend to her duties at the same time. Although it was slightly inconvenient to have to fly to Belfast for one day, at least it meant she was able to find room for both facets of her life without neglecting either.

Angus and Alexandra were learning well how to cope with this dilemma. The later sad breakdown of Princess Margaret's marriage, was in part due to the reluctance of Lord Snowdon to take part in his wife's engagements. Princess Margaret needed the reassurance of her public life, and the respect that she was shown, and as a result there was a tension between the desire for a normal family life, and the pressure of having to do what was expected in the way of public service.

The arrangements the Ogilvys had agreed upon ensured the smooth running of their marriage, and as Alexandra gained a reputation for never letting anyone down, she never received the 'bad press' of Princess Margaret which only served to worsen the situation.

But although Alexandra had definite ideas about her sense of duty, it was out of consideration for her husband and her son that she refused to accept an invitation from the Australians to become their Governor-General, a position offered to her father before the Second World War. Much as she loved Australia, and perhaps welcomed their unstuffy approach to official business, she was aware that accepting the appointment would mean that Angus could not have continued with his own career. In any case, Alexandra was too popular to be allowed out of her own country, for she was fulfilling a large number of engagements each year.

Free weekends were very rare, and it was no doubt with a sense of relief that she escaped with Angus for a few days in Perthshire, to attend the baptism of Angus's niece at Airlie Castle. They were driving past Perth, when they came across a serious accident on the road ahead of them. Angus at once stopped his own car and offered to help, and when an ambulance arrived, he insisted on travelling with the injured victims to the hospital. When he reached the hospital he asked for a police escort to look after Alexandra, who had remained at the scene of the accident, but she had already driven ahead, and arrived soon afterwards and collected her husband from the hospital. Although the Ogilvys were now several hours late, Angus shrugged off his kindness remarking that anyone would have done the same. Whether or not they would is another matter, but it was a gesture which typified the thoughtfulness of Angus, and the kind of private help he would give which was rarely publicized.

Other incidents also typified Angus's rarely publicized selflessness. The chauffeur who had often driven Alexandra when she was living at Kensington Palace had moved with her to Richmond, and now drove Angus to the City every day. On the way home from a night out once, when the Ogilvys were abroad, he crashed his car, and was subsequently disqualified from driving. Far from being furious when he returned, Angus was determined that the man's life would not be ruined because of the incident, and kept in touch with him, in the hope of giving him help. Eventually he found the man another job in the City. It was deeds like this which helped inspire the tremendous loyalty to Angus felt by all those who knew him.

Although reluctant to accompany the Princess on engagements, partly because of having to do a job, but also because he insists quite wrongly that he is no good at talking to the man in the street, Angus has always willingly accompanied the Princess on official business when he could see himself being a professional asset. For that reason, he went with Alexandra to a British Exhibition in Tokyo in 1965.

They left London as the public face of the biggest export drive ever launched from Britain into the Japanese market, an event which had taken over three years to organize. Over ten million pounds' worth of British goods from four hundred companies had preceded them, ranging from Rolls-Royce cars to chemicals and textiles, and it was expected that Alexandra's presence at the exhibition would draw crowds to view the stands.

It was an added bonus to have Angus there, as both a royal celebrity and a British businessman, and he greatly impressed the Japanese with his sensible ideas and sound knowledge of commerce. But being together also caused occasional problems for Alexandra and Angus. British protocol dictated that Alexandra should be followed by her husband at several paces distance, something which the Japanese could not understand when the couple arrived to lunch with the Emperor Hirohito at his palace. A heated argument followed when the officials tried to persuade Angus to enter first, according to Japanese etiquette. The problem was only solved when it was realized that the Princess, as the Emperor's chief guest, had precedence over Angus.

More embarrassing was the moment when Alexandra, about to make a visit to an orphanage, discovered that she had to remove her shoes. Rather taken aback, she looked somewhat bewildered for a moment at the long line of sandals which were considered acceptable, and asked, 'Which ones are for me?' It was explained that the shoes were designed to fit any foot, and the Princess tactfully stepped into the nearest pair. Any awkwardness was quickly forgotten when she saw the welcome the forty tiny children gave her inside. They waved Japanese and British flags, and after talking to many of them, Alexandra inspected the home. When she finally left, the children called out in English, 'Goodbye Princess', a difficult phrase they had been practising for weeks, and the children bowed so low that their foreheads nearly touched the ground. Alexandra could scarcely restrain a smile, but just managed to keep within the solemn Japanese etiquette.

The British Exhibition was thoroughly successful, and after brief visits to Hong Kong, Tehran and Amman, the Ogilvys returned to London via Jerusalem and Malta.

On returning home, they were met by their chauffeur in a Rolls-Royce, which was a new aquisition. Previously Angus had owned an old Jaguar, which had acquired a certain notoriety after several minor accidents. Alexandra still drove an old Mini, a left-over from the Kensington Palace days, and when she was seen in it, Angus received many letters accusing him of being mean, by not buying his wife a better car.

Previously, when the Ogilvys had required a Rolls-Royce for functions, they had simply hired one, for they disliked ostentation and had found their own vehicles satisfactory for their needs. But as hire costs increased, they had decided to buy a Rolls-Royce, not a new one, but a ten-year-old model, which in 1965 would have cost about £1,500.

There was another reason why increased comfort was important, for it was announced in the New Year that the Princess was expecting her second child in July. The news was made public after Alexandra visited her cousin King Constantine and his wife in Greece, and apart from a short stay in Amsterdam, when she was a witness at the wedding of Princess Beatrice of the Netherlands and Claus von Amsberg, Alexandra undertook no further engagements.

On the last day of July, the Ogilvys happiness was complete when a baby daughter was born. As before, Alexandra was attended by the Queen's physician, and this time, Marina, as the baby was to be called, arrived more or less on time.

All progressed well, and soon Alexandra was fit to travel again. In September, the Ogilvys spent a quiet holiday with friends in Rome, leaving the baby and James in the capable hands of Nurse Rattle. Their departure for Italy was simply as 'Mr and Mrs Ogilvy', and they travelled by economy class. The reporters, who were initially surprised to learn that they often travelled without any red carpet treatment, and as 'Mr and Mrs Kent', had by now become wise to this habit, and this time were quick enough to catch them leaving Heathrow airport.

The next important family event was the baptism of their daughter on 9 November. Angus was suffering from a bout of influenza, and had a temperature of over 100° as he struggled to the Chapel Royal at St

James's Palace with his two-year-old son. This time, the names chosen came from Marina's family. The baby was baptized Marina Victoria Alexandra, and the godparents included Princess Margaret.

The choice of St James's Palace, rather than the expected one of the private chapel of Buckingham Palace, had surprised some, but it was decided upon partly because the Ogilvys had held their wedding reception there, and also because the couple did not envisage that their daughter would in the future take any part in public life. The young girl was given a memorable and a royal start to life, and one which reflected the happiness, popularity and pride of the now well-established family into which she was lucky enough to be born.

# 17

# *Public Life*

BEFORE LONG PRINCESS ALEXANDRA was back in the throes of public duty, this time to inspect a new building which had been added to Lancaster University since her first visit there. She is still remembered with affection by the staff, who recall Alexandra's concern for news of their own children. In the Senior Common Room she would happily discuss problems of small babies, with Marina on her mind, and was always relaxed and charming.

Ironically, the students obviously had their own idea of royalty that was far more old-fashioned. The Students' Union had arranged a ball at Morecambe, and had chosen six officials to partner Alexandra at the event. Their names were submitted to Alexandra, and the chosen few hurriedly took dancing lessons. The Students' Union were rather taken aback when the Princess's Comptroller wrote in reply and noted more democratically that 'Her Royal Highness does not wish her partners to be pre-determined. She has expressed the wish that she should be free to choose her partners from the students who ask to dance. They should be brought to her in the sitting out area.'

The news was received with nervous enthusiasm, but the local ballroom class found it was overwhelmed with an unusual rush for lessons.

The Princess's attitude to students was perhaps more surprisingly shared by her mother Princess Marina, who was the Chancellor of the University of Kent. She also wanted to try to understand students by sharing their more spontaneous approach. A group from the university were invited to meet Marina at Kensington Palace, an honour which threw those invited into a panic of nerves. Urgent requests were made for advice on 'how to behave', and horrible stories spread about the sacrifice of long hair. But the normally fastidious Marina stated that she wanted the young people to come to Kensington Palace dressed as they wished, and were told not to worry about any complicated protocol they imagined to dominate the place. It was unusual, but not out of keeping with Marina's nature, for, like her daughter, she was anxious about the welfare of youth.

Alexandra, of course, believed ever more in the importance of family life as her own children grew older, and timed her engagements to coincide as far as possible with their term-time. However, she continued to make visits abroad, always evoking affection wherever she went.

After devoting several years to the same countries, revisiting them often, because she was always asked back, it was surprising that it was not until October 1967 that Alexandra made her first official visit to the United States of America. She and Angus were mainly involved in promoting a British fortnight at the Neiman-Marcus store in Dallas, Texas. Alexandra examined the displays of goods, from umbrellas to Union Jacks, but drew the line at drinking a glass of British beer which was offered to her. After Texas, another British Week followed in Toronto, where she proved too much for an old man whom she spoke to during dinner. He burst into tears, while Alexandra obligingly touched his arm in a comforting gesture, and while his wife grinned uncaringly at the observant cameras.

The long rounds of British Weeks, examining endless stands of British produce, must have been extremely taxing for Alexandra and Angus. The experience must have been much the same, from country to country, and from week to week, but by now Alexandra had learned to cope with any such situation with great skill, and if she was fed up with having to always smile and always appear interested, she never showed it.

The following year, Alexandra set off for another British Week, this time in Sweden. At least it had the merit of a little variety of location, and when the Princess arrived at Stockholm, she was confronted by a line of reporters, waiting with notebooks in hand to interview her.

Officials in Alexandra's party explained the rule that the British royal family never gave interviews, something which the Swedish Press, who would often speak to their own monarch, could not understand. The atmosphere became very tense until Alexandra, with characteristic ease, settled the matter in her own way. She tactfully shook hands with the reporters, who were obliged to leave their notebooks on a table, and instead of being interviewed proceeded to question the press about their own work, and surprised them with her considerate understanding.

117

There was nothing that Alexandra could do, for although many of the rules for guidance were unwritten they were binding.

The Press Attaché at the British Embassy later explained to the reporters that 'royalty in Britain is surrounded by a certain magic which one would not like to miss'. Nevertheless, the Swedish press felt that the British Week would have had twice the amount of publicity if the magic of British royalty had been lifted a little. They recognized that Alexandra had a great gift for public relations, but this only increased their considerable annoyance that she was isolated in a way that was unknown to the Swedes.

It was a sad misunderstanding, for of course Alexandra was noted for her love of informality. She had made many innovations, and had perhaps gone as far in her interpretation of the 'common touch' as anyone could, without being over-familiar or losing the aura of royalty demanded of her.

A British opinion poll showed that Alexandra was one of the few members of the royal family who had scored 'nil' for arrogance. Because of her personality, she was in greater demand than ever, especially as many organizations privately expressed the hope that they would not have Princess Margaret, who had a reputation for unpredictable behaviour. Alexandra also had to take on some of her cousin's workload because at the time Princess Margaret was suffering strain and great unhappiness because of the breakdown of her marriage. It was upsetting for Princess Margaret to be so often reminded of how good Alexandra was at her job, and perhaps understandable that she herself would often suggest Alexandra's name for a job with the remark, 'Let Alexandra do that; she's so good at these little things.'

Consequently, Alexandra was as busy as ever, and many of the engagements were repeats, such as the time when Alexandra launched as many as four ships in one month. She remarked, 'They should call me Helen of Troy. Wasn't she the girl who launched a thousand ships?'

It was always important that the royal family should not be involved in any political controversy, either at home or abroad, and her programme of engagements was always chosen with care, to avoid the possible attachment of any 'label' due to some apparent partiality. But from time to time problems arose. Early in March 1968, the Ogilvys were due to fly to the Mauritius Islands, to represent the Queen at the islands' independence celebrations. Everything had been packed, and the couple were ready to leave by plane, when it was announced that the visit had been cancelled. Alexandra was told that the Mauritius Islands were in a state of emergency because of violent race riots, and that there was the strong possibility that her life would be in danger if she went there. Alexandra had no choice but to accept the instructions, but she did go there the following year, and met conditions that gave an indication of the earlier trouble when she was greeted with mass demonstrations, and protesters calling 'Go home, Alexandra. We don't want you.' She represented to the Militant Movement of Mauritius, who had staged the unrest, a colonial power which they felt had exploited their country.

It was one of the few occasions when she encountered any unpleasantness, and of course she normally made such a success of any visit that she was invaluable to her family and her country. For many years, Princess Marina had watched Alexandra's career with interest and pride. Often when she visited countries after Alexandra had paid an official visit, she heard glowing reports and stories about her daughter. This was especially apparent in Australia, when Princess Marina was at last able to visit the country herself. If circumstances had been different, of course, she would have lived there as wife of the Governor-General, as her husband had been offered the post shortly before his death. When Alexandra's extraordinarily successful tour in Australia in 1959 had been reported to Marina, she wrote to a friend

I am indeed overwhelmed with pride about Alexandra possessing the wonderful gift of spreading happiness around her. It has made her tour something greater than a triumph, and is very moving for me.

Now ten years later, she could look back on her words as a prophecy. It was, of course, largely due to Marina herself that Alexandra had developed such a rich personality, and as Alexandra grew into maturity, her thoughts must have turned to her mother. Throughout years of early widowhood, Marina never shirked the often gruelling duty she performed for her adopted country. It had never been easy for her as a Greek Princess with her own ideas, and at the start she had very few friends of her own. Sadly, she had never quite been accepted by some members of the royal family, who regarded her with slight suspicion. Although she had a powerful personality, Marina was by nature extremely shy, and found it difficult to press for changes which would benefit herself or her family. Perhaps this was most apparent when she asked to be allowed by the royal family to sell off some of her late husband's objets d'art. No provision had been made for her after the Duke of Kent's death, and it was clear that the Princess had very little income to devote to her family and household. But her own suffering only encouraged her understanding of others in need, and despite her own lack of wealth she never grudged what financial help she could offer to others. Her kindness to a family who had been left penniless after the Russian Revolution, whom she partly supported, and her provision of a rent-free cottage to another family of Polish refugees left bereft after the Second World War, are little known.

In later years, after her family had married, she never reduced her calendar of engagements, and compensated for her loneliness by absorbing herself in her favourite pastime of painting and drawing. Friends remember delightful evenings where the company was largely drawn from the world of the arts, when she would amuse and be amused. She was, a friend said, never malicious, and would never allow herself to listen to nasty gossip. Admittedly, Marina had at times a strictness about her which slightly intimidated those who met her for the first time, but when this barrier, mainly caused by shyness, was passed, she had a delightful sense of humour, and would entertain with the exquisite manners and taste for which she was famous.

When she was in her early sixties in 1968, Marina might have been taken for a woman ten years younger, for she had never become fixed in one fashion, and continued to dress with the elegance for which she had become famous when she first arrived in Britain. She herself was surprised by the sudden inexplicable bouts of tiredness which came upon her now, and characteristically joked to her friends that she was growing old without really believing it herself. But unfortunately she was beginning to suffer the complaints of age. Of more concern was a painful left leg, which caused her to stumble unexpectedly.

Marina was a devoted tennis enthusiast, and would often attend the Wimbledon Lawn Tennis Championships. Early in July 1968 she was there, as happy and cheerful as ever, when she presented the trophies to the winners and chatted with them. It was, however, the last occasion when she was seen in public. Soon after, Marina was advised, very much against her own will, to visit a hospital for tests to find the trouble with her painful leg. A six-day examination revealed that the Princess was suffering from an inoperable brain tumour, and at the most could be expected to survive for six months.

The agonizing news was broken to Alexandra and her two brothers, but kept from Marina. Fortunately, Marina and her family were spared the ordeal of a long and painful illness. The last family event was on 25 August, when Marina and a friend received Angus and Alexandra for luncheon. Even then, Marina was in a cheerful mood, and was looking forward to her visitors, even if there was the background sadness of it being the twenty-sixth anniversary of her husband's death.

After the Ogilvys left, Marina and her friend watched a detective series on television, and Marina decided to go to bed early. She was perfectly composed, but embarrassed and annoyed when she fell while climbing the stairs to her bedroom. On the following morning, she awoke after 9 but remarked, 'I feel tired. I think I will go to sleep.'

Those were her last words, for Marina then lapsed into unconsciousness. Alexandra and her brothers were quickly sent for, and arrived to sit at their mother's bedside. Alexandra telephoned for Marina's sister, Princess Olga, to come urgently from Florence. When her sister arrived later in the evening, Marina opened her eyes briefly, but never regained consciousness.

On Tuesday 27 August, she died peacefully. The friend who had been with her felt certain that Marina knew she was going to die, and had the sense that her husband had somehow come to fetch her.

The Queen issued instructions that the late Duke of Kent's remains were to be removed from St George's Chapel, Windsor, for Marina had always disliked intensely the gloom of the Royal Vaults, and at her own wish Marina and George were interred together in the small burial ground near the mausoleum of Queen Victoria and Prince Albert. Also the burial place of the Duke of Windsor, it is a quiet and peaceful place, where Marina often used to walk with her husband.

Marina's death was a great grief to Alexandra, for she knew more than anybody how much her mother had given to her country. It was some comfort for the Kents to realize the great regard and affection that their mother had been held in. Apart from the expected heads of organizations, and official representatives, the seats of Westminster Abbey were packed with ordinary people, whose lives had been touched by Marina, and came to remember her at the Memorial Service there.

# 18

# *Friend to All*

THE ROLE OF the monarchy had changed since Marina had first taken her place in the royal family in 1934. Largely due to the war, and the breakdown of class barriers, the royal family, and especially its younger members, had to be more approachable to outsiders. A lead had come from George VI and Queen Elizabeth, who gained such popularity when they visited the East End of London during the war, and spoke to the victims of the Blitz. The King and Queen understood the suffering of their people, and when Buckingham Palace was also bombed, Queen Elizabeth remarked, 'It makes me feel I can look the East End in the face.'

But no matter how sympathetic the royal family may feel, towards the victims of social inequalities, for example, there is little they can do about it practically. The royal family are well aware of how a false face is often presented for royal visits, and how a coat of paint is applied to conceal the decay underneath, but theirs is not the job of changing such things. There are exceptions though. When the Queen happened to notice some slums from a train when passing through Leeds, she was so shocked at what she saw that she spoke to the then Prime Minister, Harold Wilson, about the housing conditions. She asked him what plans were being made to improve the area, and as a result, something was done to help.

But for other members of the family, who do not have access to the government, it is harder to make any real changes, however strongly they feel them to be necessary. When Alexandra arrived at Liverpool University to open a Senate Building and an expensive research laboratory, she was greeted with loud cat-calls and boos, instead of the usual cheers. The protest came not from student demonstrators, but from housewives, waving placards with slogans about their poor housing conditions. The tenants' association which they had formed had been unable to make any progress towards obtaining improvements from the local authority.

The noisy women continued to chant, and Alexandra was clearly upset. She broke away from her official party, and crossed the street to ask the demonstrators about their problems. She was told that the houses in question had no bathrooms, no hot water, and no internal sanitation, only dilapidated outside lavatories. Alexandra told the women that surely as the 'conditions were so unpleasant', it was 'unthinkable that in this day and age, nothing could be done to help'.

At these words, the tenants' annoyance changed to admiration for the Princess, and when she joined the university group, she was loudly cheered. One woman commented, 'When a princess says that something will be done, you can be sure it will.'

Only a week later Alexandra may well have recalled the plight of the women in Liverpool, as she unveiled a plaque to commemorate the 150th anniversary of Burlington Arcade, the luxury shopping area off Bond Street. There could be no greater contrast between the housewives and the rich shopkeepers, dressed in Regency costume, handing out champagne. No two engagements could have brought home to Alexandra so forcibly the difficulties of her position and the regard in which she was held.

As economic conditions worsened into the 1970s, greater care than before was taken with the engagements of the royal family. Alexandra's office grew more careful to avoid association with any event which gave an ostentatious or extravagant appearance, being, well aware of the kind of criticism that could be levelled at them by those suffering from genuine hardship. When it was decided to increase the Civil List allowance for the Queen, one newspaper carried a letter which grumbled, 'It's all right for them, inside the Palaces'.

Alexandra prefers to accept engagements which are close to her own interests, and with her two children and their education in mind, she enthusiastically accepted the invitation of the Corporation of the City of London to open the City of London School for Girls, which had moved to a new building in the Barbican complex near St Paul's.

After Alexandra had been welcomed by the Lord Mayor and the headmistress, she was presented with a bouquet by the head girl, and the royal party and other guests proceeded to the Assembly Hall. The school had been upset by a long series of building problems, and the girls and staff had moved into a mess of rubble and dust, but the prospect of a royal visit had encouraged the workmen to complete certain unfinished jobs quickly, and now the building presented an exciting new face to the Princess.

Alexandra said in her opening speech:

Today is, I know, an important occasion for the City of London School for Girls, and I am so very happy to be here to share it with you all. . . . The new school building is part of one of the biggest developments in the City of London, and its outline is very much of the twentieth century, but, like the Barbican itself, with its roots firmly in Roman foundations, the school remains as its founder intended, as a place for the provision of useful learning.

Alexandra also spoke of the importance of learning more than simply educational facts, and of her own belief, that '. . . It is people that matter, and the way they face the challenge of living.'

After Alexandra had unveiled the plaque, she inspected the school. In order for everything to run smoothly, the day had been rehearsed by the school like a military operation. As always on these occasions, the meticulous organization was repaid. It was a wonderful if exhausting day for the girls, and one remembered by many of them.

When the Princess left the Assembly Hall, the girls were allowed to rush into their various classrooms at a pace normally forbidden, to join those who were apparently casually involved in a project. Some girls were in the needlework room, busily 'finishing' embroidery, and as the lift door opened and Alexandra stepped out, one girl recalled,

I could feel my hands becoming hotter and hotter. . . . It was a strange thing, but when the Princess did come into the room, her natural grace and friendliness made me wonder why I had even worried. . . .

The days of preparation for Alexandra's visit were justified, and the various accounts the girls have given show how strong an impression Alexandra made on them, even on the very young, who were able to look objectively at the visit without the misty eyed rapture which sometimes accompanies adults' accounts of their meeting with royalty.

Many of the girls noted Alexandra's gift for drawing out even the most nervous from behind her shyness, and her ability to talk to complete strangers. One older girl said:

I think we would all agree that one of the chief distinguishing features of the Princess's visit was this ability to talk in a friendly informal way with one person, when faced with our necessarily somewhat regimented ranks. We felt the warmth of her interest, which made her visit much more than an official inspection.

It was an incident typical of the way that Alexandra managed to maintain a personal touch of friendliness within a rigorous programme of official events. Before making a short visit to New Zealand in April 1971, the Ogilvys invited to their home members of a club that aimed to promote understanding between the handicapped and able-bodied people. The club had completed a sponsored walk in Richmond Park, and Angus's invitation reflected his increasing concern for charitable work. As Patron for the British Rheumatism and Arthritis Association, Angus understood the need for a greater effort to help the handicapped. He could also sympathize from his own experience of suffering constantly from back trouble since his ski-ing accident, which caused him severe pain.

He had in fact met some of the members a few days previously, when a friend felt that he was rather ill at ease. Angus had never quite developed the easy, chatty manner of Alexandra. After a ten-minute conversation in Thatched House Lodge, Angus remarked that he would fetch his wife, and after Alexandra arrived he was much more relaxed, and called her 'darling' or 'sweetie'. He readily admits that he feels ill at ease talking to strangers, and has said that he is not 'one of the chaps who scrubs floors in the East End. I'm not made that way.'

During the conversation, he tried unsuccessfully to catch Alexandra's attention. She was talking to a handicapped boy, and would not come over to him. Smiling, he said to his companions 'I'm afraid she's being rather Bolshie today.' But if Angus feels that he is 'happy to raise money for charities, because money is something I know about', it is not so easy to believe him when he insists that he is '. . . not much good at chatting up the "Bloggins bit"'. Doubtless, it is a modest assessment, and one that is rather unfair; for a diary typical of that time indicates that for three months the Ogilvys attended functions so constantly that they had only one free weekend with their children. Angus was prompted to say

I think the time is coming very shortly when if we don't see a lot more of our children, we're going to pay the price at the other end, when they're older. But it's very difficult. You decide to spend an evening with the children, but then someone rings up and says, 'Will you please come to a film premiere. If you come, it will help us raise another £1,500 and this could help, say, 300 spastics.' Well, who are more important, 300 spastics, or your own children? We've got to try to get a balance which changes with the age of the children.

The problem was partly solved in 1970 when James first of all was sent to a prep school in South Kensington, and Marina a little later to one in Chelsea. It was part of Alexandra and Angus's determined policy of ensuring that the children should have a conventional upbringing, should not be ensnared in public life, and should be allowed to follow their own interests.

Alexandra's engagements continued on the home front after New Zealand, with sometimes as many as three functions to attend in one day, and perhaps a dinner party in the evening. Even for as accomplished a person as Alexandra, this could at times prove too exhausting, and in the winter of 1972 she was advised by her physicians to rest in Switzerland, for since the previous autumn she had been dogged by bronchial trouble, and had been unable to throw off a persistent cold.

The fault was partly Alexandra's, for against advice she would never retire to bed, and had insisted on keeping all her appointments. After the five-day stay originally planned in Switzerland the Princess was told that she had not responded to the Swiss climate as quickly as hoped, and had to remain abroad for a further week.

When she returned, she was looking noticeably tired, but this brief respite did little to discourage Alexandra from resuming her rigorous schedule. She left shortly afterwards for a visit to the United States, and later in the year travelled to Afghanistan, en route for Hong Kong, and back to London after a brief visit to Cyprus.

Angus, too, had been in poor health, and similarly refused to reduce his workload. When he sent for auction at Sothebys various pictures which realized £20,000, it was rumoured that he was giving up his work in the City. But this was quite untrue – he actually used the money to buy two hundred acres near Crieff in Perthshire the following year.

Although Angus had virtually become a Londoner by adoption, he never disguised the fact that he missed his own country. He always had wanted to buy a house there with sufficient land to give both Alexandra and himself the kind of privacy that they needed. Throughout the years, the heavy expenses of helping to keep his wife in the manner fitting to her station had meant that he could not afford to realize this ambition. Angus had been offered various houses, many of them quite large, but they were all rejected because of the cost. Now he decided to make the first step by buying the land, in the hope that before too long they would be able to build a modest cottage or farmhouse, with simply a couple of rooms.

The land in Perthshire was not beautiful, but would, Angus hoped, provide a place where he and Alexandra could retreat from time to time, and perhaps even retire there. For some years the land lay vacant, and the problems became painfully apparent. When Angus discussed the cost of laying pipes and other services in the land, and weighed it against the kind of use they would get from their house, they reluctantly decided that they simply would not be able to find the time to live there, and they eventually sold it.

One problem with their Richmond home was its distance from central London, which made travelling to engagements difficult, especially when Alexandra or Angus had to change for an evening function, or try to arrive on time during or around the rush hour. On one occasion, when the Ogilvys were on their way to meet a foreign V.I.P. and were seriously delayed by an accident at Chiswick, a police escort had to be sent for to get the Ogilvys through to London on time.

It was clear that to perform their duties efficiently and without harassment, the Ogilvys would need to change to another home, and when they were offered a rent-free house in Hyde Park by the Queen, the problem seemed to be solved. Known as the Ranger's Lodge, the house had stood empty for many years, and would require complete renovation to make it habitable.

However, the announcement that the Ogilvys were to be given a free house caused an instant storm of abuse. Anti-royalist M.P. William Hamilton remarked, 'There is no reason why they should be given this privilege.' The reaction was aggravated by the timing of the offer by the Queen, which coincided with a similar complaint that the Army had provided a house for Princess and Captain Mark Phillips for a rent of only £8 per week.

In many ways, the house in Hyde Park was larger than the Ogilvys wanted, for they had really felt that even a two-roomed flat in central London would be adequate to help them out, and if this had been available, they could have kept their Richmond home. But as the cost of repairing the house in Hyde Park was so great, Angus indicated that it would cost far more than he could afford, and that he and Alexandra did not think it was fair to expect the country to pay for it either. Living at a time of mass unemployment and housing shortage, finally persuaded them to decline the offer, and they soldiered on with their duties from the base of Thatched House Lodge.

# 19

# *Charity Work*

THERE HAD BEEN many innovations to the public image of royalty during the Queen's reign, with the intention of updating its role without losing any of the mystique. No one has done more to bring the monarchy into the twentieth century than Prince Philip, who himself has said,

We are constantly adapting to changing circumstances but these changes are seldom big enough in themselves to attract attention. Many of the more obvious ceremonial activities remain the same because we have reason to believe that people enjoy such things as the Changing of the Guard. . . . At the same time, a number of other activities such as the Presentation Parties [for debutantes] have been done away with. There have also been a number of initiatives. For example the old bombed Chapel at Buckingham Palace has been converted into a picture exhibition gallery. We have regular and informal luncheon and dinner parties. . . .

The royal family had also been able to let the passage of time dim the shock and consequences of the abdication of Edward VIII in 1936, a sign of the new relaxed protocol. The Queen invited the Duke of Windsor and his wife to an unveiling of a plaque to his mother, Queen Mary in 1966. Even between generations a substantial change of attitudes was evident, for which the Duke of Windsor was, as it were, a touchstone. Alexandra had often visited her uncle and his wife when she was in Paris, but it was something Marina refused to do. Shortly after the abdication, the Duke of Windsor found himself staying near Marina and her husband, and invited the Kents to visit him and the Duchess of Windsor. Marina would not meet the former Mrs Simpson, and so the Duke of Kent was obliged to decline the invitation.

It was possibly only in this century, and particularly after the Second World War, that circumstances made it possible for a commoner such as Angus to marry a royal princess. The success of their marriage, obvious to all, set a precedent which was extremely helpful in preparing the way for Captain Mark Philips' engagement to Princess Anne. Indeed, it was a fitting coincidence that Princess Anne and her husband spent the first night of their honeymoon at Thatched House Lodge.

The Ogilvys' circumstances changed dramatically in the midsummer of 1976 when, after an upheaval in the City, Angus resigned his business directorships. There was no obligation for him to do so, and it was eventually proved that Angus could not be blamed in any way, but a situation had arisen which might eventually have proved embarrassing to the royal family, and he preferred to more or less withdraw from the City to avoid even the risk of bad publicity. Of course attention was especially focused on Angus, purely because of his unique position, and his exoneration was well received, but there were more important consequences which went largely unnoticed, principally the fact that his decision meant a drastic cut in his income. It was only as a result of this change that they themselves could discern just how much of Angus's income had gone towards supporting his wife, and how inadequate was Alexandra's allowance. Angus refused to draw the Queen's attention to the problem, however, for he felt that pride would not allow him to beg money, and he had after all worked hard to achieve all that he had earned. But something had to be done to cope with their new circumstances. Angus had borrowed heavily to buy the Richmond home, and for a time there was the danger that they would have to sell it. The small amount of inherited wealth he had received had been used up, so there was only one option left. It was then that the Perthshire land was sold. He told a reporter:

People used to say I was always determined that my wife would only fulfil her duties in the best and most proper style. Frankly, I'd be delighted if there was some way we could do it on the cheap. My wife and I are not really Rolls-Royce people, and are quite happy with a Jaguar. . . .

Throughout these difficulties, Alexandra was unswervingly loyal to her husband, and concerned that it was because of her own position that his City connection had received so much attention. It was not surprising that Angus was soon suffering from pneumonia, and had to enter the King Edward VII Hospital for a much-needed rest.

In some respects, the change of circumstances was a blessing in disguise, for it meant that Angus would have to put up less with the previous strain and anxiety. He devoted more of his time to working for charity, and when he was appointed a director of Sothebys, the auctioneers, as their roving ambassador, he was able to put to effective and enjoyable use his extensive knowledge of fine art.

Later in 1976 attention was focused more interestingly on another Ogilvy (or more correctly, Ogilvie) an ancestor who was a Catholic martyr executed in the seventeenth century. John Ogilvie had been firstly declared 'Venerable' in 1929 and then the Archbishop of Glasgow began the process of Beatification. In Scotland a man whose doctors had declared his cancer incurable had invoked the intercession of Ogilvie, and it was believed that his subsequent miraculous cure was in answer to this prayer.

Strictly speaking, two miracles are required before canonization, but as the sick man's recovery was so strikingly beyond all medical explanation, the Pope began the process of making Ogilvie a saint, a process which culminated in a Vatican service in 1976.

Angus and Alexandra, along with other members of the Ogilvy family, were present at this ceremony at the Vatican, and during Mass Alexandra and her family inadvertently received Roman Catholic Communion. Immediately this was noticed a scandal broke out, for it was then a strict rule, since relaxed under special circumstances, that non-Roman Catholics may not receive communion from the Roman Church. In fact this digression was entirely unintended; communion had been dispensed so rapidly that the family had not time to consider what was happening, and when Alexandra heard of the error, she was extremely upset.

The Princess could not, however, be blamed for the misunderstandings, more or less ludicrous, which inevitably resulted from her duties from time to time. In August 1977, for instance, Alexandra went to Bognor Regis, and part of her schedule included the unveiling of a plaque marking the opening of a new entertainment centre. The plaque was set in a tall brick wall, and only two days after the ceremony, the local ratepayers were astonished to notice that the entire wall including the plaque had been completely demolished. It was discovered that not a brick of the actual complex had been laid, and that Alexandra had simply been asked to unveil the plaque on the 'occasional' wall because her presence would, in the words of the council, 'help the centre to get off the ground', Alexandra's visit was too good not to make use of.

Be that as it may, the Council had certainly put the Princess in what turned out to be a potentially embarrassing situation. Alexandra could make no comment, and even worse was the unnecessary waste of her time, including meaningless gestures, in an always busy schedule.

It seemed a time for embarrassment, for when Alexandra attended a rock concert given by Elton John soon after, a trivial incident was blown out of all proportion and the unfair publicity only irritated Alexandra. She had come to like Elton John's music through her children's influence, and so was glad to attend the concert which was held in aid of the Silver Jubilee Fund. Most of the audience was unusually in black tie, and Elton John himself was so nervous that he forgot some of his words, but the concert was an outstanding success, raising nearly £30,000. Afterwards, Elton John was presented to Princess Alexandra, and red faces were caused by his later publicizing their conversation, especially the fact that Alexandra had asked the singer whether he took cocaine. John remarked that the Princess was astonished that he was able to play for two-and-a-half-hours at a stretch, without some sort of stimulant.

The singer remarked that he was stunned at Alexandra's question, and hoped that she would not be embarrassed by his publicizing her remarks. When Alexandra heard about his reaction, she was typically apologetic, and took the trouble to write to Elton John, explaining that her awkward question had slipped out during a lull in the conversation, and that she admired him very much.

If anyone could possibly argue from these uncharacteristic incidents that there is little point in many of the functions that the Princess undertakes, they certainly would be contradicted by the obviously immense value of her work for the various charities with which she is involved, either as Patron or through some other association. As the years passed, she undertook more and more of this type of work. From the earliest days, when Alexandra made her first public appearance alone with the Junior Red Cross, she had never lost her involvement with the organization. Often appearing at their events, she, perhaps more than anybody else, encouraged interest in the plight of the handicapped at a time when they were largely ignored.

In the public mind the Red Cross evokes an image of first aid enthusiasts, but its services are broader than that one aspect of its work. One of the tasks the organization undertook was to give aid to the Vietnamese 'boat people', the war refugees who sailed away from their country in the late 1970s. When Alexandra was in Hong Kong in 1980, she made a special visit to the Kai Tak refugee camp, where the Red

Cross were working under great difficulties and had almost given up hope of success. When Alexandra, one of the Vice-Presidents, learned of this, she spent a long time discussing the problems with the camp's officers, offering advice and encouragement, which was appreciated so much that the whole venture was given a new lease of life.

More remarkable, she was able to help in a positive way in Hong Kong by improving the social position of women to some extent.'For a variety of reasons, blind women were on the bottom of the social and economic ladder around the world. Alexandra, as President of the Royal Commonwealth Society for the Blind, made a habit of contacting the Society's representative in advance of any visit she might make to a Commonwealth country.

Before this visit, she had heard of a blind woman, Miss Lucy Ching, living in Hong Kong, and made a special point of meeting her after she arrived. Alexandra then ensured that Miss Ching was invited to some official event that she herself attended in Hong Kong. Miss Ching was thus seen to be socially acceptable, and Alexandra's help gave her enormous confidence. Eventually, she became a senior civil servant in the Hong Kong Government, something she could not have achieved had Alexandra not helped her, and by so doing made the position of blind women more respectable. Her help made a real contribution towards changing attitudes, and far more quickly than might have otherwise been possible.

Her interest and support were recognized by the Society in 1979, when the Chairman of the Council told Alexandra at a meeting 'how greatly we appreciate all you have done for this Society, both at home and overseas'.

The reply Alexandra made showed how much the Society's work meant to her. She spoke movingly and knowledgeably of the remarkable achievement of restoring sight to over six hundred thousand people in the Indian sub-continent, and of 'the blind people who are living testimonials of the support and encouragement given to them by the Royal Commonwealth Society for the Blind'.

# 20

# *Warmth and Enthusiasm*

IT IS NOT difficult to see why Alexandra is regarded as one of the most sympathetic members of the royal family. Like Queen Elizabeth the Queen Mother, she is quite natural with others who are from different backgrounds. There is never any indication of condescension in what Alexandra says to others, and it is her understanding nature, which characteristically makes her the confidante of her brothers and their wives, which has won her so many friends. She remains the linchpin of her family. When the Duchess of Kent suffered severe depression after the loss of her baby in 1979, it was Alexandra, a tower of strength, who did most to encourage her sister-in-law to struggle her way back to fitness.

Alexandra was delighted when she heard that her brother Michael had found happiness at last, and wanted to marry the former interior designer, Baroness Marie Christine Von Reiburg. But it was a problematical marriage to arrange, for the thirty-three-year-old Baroness was a divorcee, and from a Roman Catholic family. She wished to marry Prince Michael in her own church, but in order to do so a Papal dispensation was necessary.

The Apostolic Delegate, it seemed, had promised this would be granted, and arrangements were made for a church wedding in Vienna, but only two weeks before the actual day of the wedding, the couple were distressed to learn that the dispensation had not been granted after all.

The reason for the Pope's refusal was probably that Prince Michael had indicated that any children of the marriage would be instructed in the Anglican Faith, and would only receive an understanding of Roman Catholicism. The Privy Council had asked Michael to make these conditions before they would agree to his marriage, and even then he had given up his place in the royal succession in order to be allowed to marry a Roman Catholic at all. His hands were tied, for if he had agreed to the demand of the Apostolic Delegate to bring up any children as Roman Catholics, the Privy Council might have invoked their control over royal matches and refused consent to his marriage. It was also a distressing time for the Baroness, who was anxious to have her marriage recognized by her own church.

Although a compromise it was with a tremendous sense of relief that the couple were at last able to marry in a private civil ceremony in Austria on 30 June 1978. They were joined by Angus and Alexandra in Vienna, and also Lord Mountbatten, the Duke of Kent, Lady Helen Windsor and Princess Anne. Although the Queen was unable to be present, she had approved the style and title for the new princess of 'Her Royal Highness', something which had been denied to the Duchess of Windsor, also a divorcee, forty years earlier.

Princess Michael, as she prefers to be known, settled very quickly in the royal family, and took up her duties with an enthusiasm that is said to have surprised the Queen. There were even suggestions that she was vying for popularity with Princess Alexandra, but if that was the impression she gave, her efforts might be attributed to over-enthusiasm.

There never has been any lessening for the demand for Alexandra. In 1979, for example, she made fifty official visits, attended eleven receptions or luncheons, held four audiences, and undertook four overseas visits. Even this awesome tally of functions gives no indication of the actual amount of work involved, for one visit might include twenty engagements, and countless handshakes.

In 1980 there was no slackening of her pace, and early in the New Year, Alexandra was asked to present twelve children of courage with awards given by a woman's magazine in Westminster Abbey. It was a bitterly cold day, and most of the children were tongue-tied with nerves until they saw Alexandra arrive in her cheerful pink coat, trimmed with fur. Various toy companies had donated their products for the children, and celebrities such as Terry Scott added to the occasion. One small boy had rescued his brother from a chimney, but perhaps the most touching of those who received the awards was a tiny girl who suffered from spina bifida, and had overcome great obstacles, and pain, and taught herself to walk.

Near the end of the year Alexandra planned a visit to Australia, to mark the centenary celebrations of the Melbourne Exhibition Building in October. Before she left England, however, an embarrassing political row blew up there between the Prime Minister, Mr Fraser, and the leader of the opposition, Mr Hayden.

The royal visit had nothing to do with politics, of course, and Alexandra's engagements were to end three days before the Australian general election. Mr Fraser, however, was afraid that Mr Hayden would make Alexandra's visit a political issue, and wanted the opposition leader's assurance that this would not happen, warning that if necessary he was prepared to postpone Alexandra's visit. Hayden replied that he felt members of the royal family should not be present during an election campaign, but agreed to cause no controversy provided he was allowed the use of an official aeroplane which had been reserved for Alexandra's use.

Alexandra herself sent a message indicating that she would understand if alteration to the schedule had to be made, but in fact in the absence of any change she decided to travel, and was even given a much better aeroplane than the one originally intended.

When Alexandra had last visited Australia in 1978, she had carried out fifty-two engagements in fifteen days, without any rest, and although she enjoyed herself, many of her party felt that they were on their knees with exhaustion. The 1980 tour was therefore planned to be less hectic, but as one commentator remarked

Knowing the Princess as I do, in all the places in her programme which say 'no official engagements', she will probably fill them up. She enters into everything so marvellously, and she loves Australia!

Alexandra was accompanied by Angus, with his valet, her Lady-in-Waiting, her secretary and her maid. They were met by Mr Fraser, and the Governor-General, Sir Zelman Cowen. The visit was still dogged by political squabbling. Fraser had agreed not to be seen with Alexandra more than once, in case he was accused of making political capital out of her visit, and so certain alterations had been made to Alexandra's plans. Mr Hayden did not attend the official reception for the royal party at Canberra, because he wanted the visit to be as low-key as possible. Despite all this, the crowd at the airport clearly thought otherwise, cheering with great excitement when Alexandra and Angus walked over to talk with some of them.

Early in the tour Alexandra went to a home for juvenile offenders in Cartin, near Canberra. Tea was provided for the Ogilvys in the garden and when someone noticed that there was no lemon for Alexandra's tea, a small boy was sent to his home for the missing item. Delighted by the kind thought, Alexandra asked to meet her messenger. The boy was impressed, but not overwhelmed. 'I've seen her on television,' he said cheerfully.

The forgotten lemon was of course quite trivial, but it seemed to symbolize the start of several hitches which threatened to spoil the Ogilvys' tour. First, plans for a half-day public holiday on the day of their visit to the Melbourne Exhibition Buildings had to be cancelled, because it was feared the break would inordinately disrupt industry. Then, various events which the chairman and his committee of the centenary celebrations had taken months to organize were dropped for reasons of economy, a decision which caused much annoyance and disappointment. To add to the problems, council workers had gone on strike, and refused to remove rubbish, including thousands of empty beer cans which had piled up outside the new buildings. Other employees were asked to clear the mess, but their trade unions forbade this, and as the dispute escalated there was a threat that pickets would try to prevent the royal visitors from entering the Exhibition Buildings.

The strikers demands for more money was quickly settled in time, but matters were still less than amicable and only Alexandra could have saved the actual day, in the midst of so much ill feeling. Her efforts exceeded even the organizers expectations, for looking her most attractive in a light blue suede dress, with matching hat, Alexandra was completely relaxed in the sweltering heat as she arrived at the Exhibition Building. She was obviously keener on talking to the visiting groups of children than to the important platform party who were waiting to receive her. The officials were unprepared when a small girl, excited and happy, called out in awe, 'Are you really a princess?' At once uniformed attendants rushed forward to remove the noisy culprit, but she was quite unabashed, and Alexandra did not want to disappoint the child, and stopped to talk to her. The girl ran off yelling loudly, 'She is, she is a princess!'

All the early upsets were forgotten as Alexandra, with her usual instinct for the right thing to do, broke away from her party to look at the stands which were not on her schedule, and to talk to quite ordinary bystanders. The feeble protests of security men were waved aside, and Alexandra assured them, 'There's no need to worry.' Alexandra was, as so often, quite unstoppable. One moment she surprised a few medical students, dressed in shorts and short-sleeved shirts who had hurried out between lectures to have a quick look round; next, she had gone over to talk to a mixed school choir, who had greeted her arrival with a song. The description the Princess gave to the building in her opening speech as 'an inspired mixture of dignity and panache' might well have applied to herself. And suitably, the building acquired the additional title of 'Royal', a present which Alexandra gave on behalf of the Queen.

Later in the tour, while visiting Victoria, the Princess paid a tribute to her old friend, the late Sir Robert Menzies, by opening a National Federation of Fitness and Physical Achievement which bore his name. Alexandra remarked that the former Prime Minister had welcomed her to Australia 'further back than I care to remember', and she had asked Sir Robert to be godfather to her son James, and was grateful for the chance to pay tribute to his memory. She was certain, she said, that the Foundation would keep his name as a 'shining example which will live forever in the land he loved.'

But more problems were in store. When the Princess and Angus arrived in Portland, they were due to inspect a meat market, and the premises were duly scrubbed and tidied up. However, employees had decided to work a four-day week, and their day off coincided with the royal visit. Accordingly, the plans were hastily altered, and the Ogilvys went to a local hospital, and, to spin out the time, a nearby harbour.

Troubles were not over yet, for the opposition leader, Mr Hayden, declined an invitation to attend a state reception for Alexandra and Angus, a decision which was interpreted as a snub to the royal visitors.

In pleasant contrast, Angus and Alexandra spent a weekend on the Prime Minister's farm before continuing their visit in Adelaide. There, Alexandra and Angus visited a new Festival Centre, and Alexandra made an impromptu tour of the kitchens. She later arrived on the stage, where the company was rehearsing *Bent*, a play about Nazi persecution of homosexuals in concentration camps in the last war. Alexandra chatted to two 'SS' officers, and an actor who was playing the part of a 'transvestite'. She moved quickly out of the way, when photographs were taken, but Angus remained undisturbed, apparently unconcerned at any association with an often taboo subject.

Alexandra's visit to Alice Springs was new territory, and she obviously welcomed the chance to see Australia's famous beauty spot. She was primarily there to open a new railway, but on the day of the ceremony decided to explore the area in a novel way. Early in the morning she and Angus were lent bicycles, and, unobserved, covered a large area of countryside before returning for breakfast. Alexandra remarked that she often used to cycle at home with her son, and was grateful for the exercise, especially after having to sit through several receptions. Angus was less sure, for he 'hadn't ridden a bicycle for about thirty years, and I was terrified that I'd fall off'.

Transport of a different kind took up the Ogilvys' attention in the afternoon. A disused railway line at Alice Springs had been repaired for a new service, which it was hoped would increase tourism to the area. The local schoolchildren had been given the day off, and when the train moved slowly to the reception point, they waved flags and cheered. To general jubilation, Alexandra had driven the engine for the last few yards, and a band played 'She'll be coming round the mountain' as the train arrived, and Alexandra declared the line open.

Alice Springs had been the scene of one of Australia's most publicized mysteries, when in early 1980 a small baby had met a strange death, allegedly the victim of a dingo, the Australian wild dog. Despite modern scepticism, the awesome legend had deterred many a potential visitor, and well aware of the reputation the area had acquired, Alexandra made an unplanned visit to the place to satisfy curiosity. Dressed in casual clothes, and obviously quite calm, her relaxed visit was seen by millions on television, and helped to bring the visitors back to Ayres Rock. In fact, the mystery was cleared up soon after. After several reports providing evidence from forensic experts, as late as early 1982 the parents were suddenly arrested, and charged with the murder of their daughter.

Alexandra had now visited Australia four times, and had often covered the same ground. The protests that occurred during the 1980 tour were not directed at her personally, but were, as usual, trying to use her presence to gain publicity for their own cause. Even so, none of the visits had been quite so testing for Alexandra, for apart from the political rows, there were suggestions that the expense incurred did not justify the Ogilvys' visit. The press hinted that Alexandra had been to Australia too often for her presence to be even interesting. One only had to follow her tour to know otherwise – it was a theory which was not shared by those she met.

Popular opinion was summed up in a paper which said, after the Ogilvys had returned to England:

Princess Alexandra and her husband, Angus Ogilvy have . . . left behind a trail of warmth and enthusiasm. Alexandra. who first won the hearts of Australians during her 1959 tour, did it again: friendly, chatting, laughing, or thoughtful, she appeared to enjoy herself. . . . It's a long time between tours, but Your [Royal] Highness, it was nice seeing you.

# EPILOGUE

# *Alexandra the Greatest*

As PRINCESS ALEXANDRA approaches early middle age, there is no lessening of her popularity, and every sign that she will continue to give pleasure, encouragement and kindness to those whom she meets for many years to come. In fact, few could complain if she decided to withdraw gradually from the limelight, for as younger members of the royal family grow up, and gradually take their place in public service, there are more people available to do the job. When Alexandra began, she was almost alone, with only the Queen and Princess Margaret to be counted among the younger members of the royal family. But since then the numbers have increased, and it might be argued that Alexandra deserves a rest, to have more time with her family, and to enjoy the quiet years she has earned by such hard work. But as a close friend has said, 'There is no question of Alexandra giving up, for as long as she is still wanted, she will continue with her public life.'

Alexandra's success as a member of the royal family, and often being the one who is liked by anti-royalists, is partly due to her happy marriage, and also to her genuinely modest assessment of her own talents. She finds it difficult to believe that she has done anything at all that could be worth writing about.

When Alexandra married Angus Ogilvy, critics suggested that the admittance of a commoner to an exclusive institution would somehow destroy the sense of mystique which makes the British monarchy so buoyant. By bringing to the royal family part of the outside world which had never touched them before, it was suggested that he was lowering the monarchy and bringing it down to a level which was understood too clearly by the man in the street for it to have any appeal.

Rather than dragging down the monarchy, though, Angus has at times brought new ideas which have refreshed the image of royalty, and indeed provided just the right sort of link between his everyday world and the rather exclusive world of the monarchy.

In recent years, he has given more of his time to charity, using his sound business knowledge to real advantage, and along with the down to earth approach of his wife, the Ogilvys helped, rather than hindered, the monarchy, by hitting just the right note of charm and royal dignity. Alexandra's admirers have found in her the exact combination of the image of 'royalty' with genuine humility, which has made her approachable and human. It might be written off as a sign of the times, but in truth it is also a sign of Alexandra's influence. Her grandmother, Queen Mary, for example, was exactly the opposite; intensely regal, she never wanted to reduce the barriers between her own personality and the public, but was content to be loved simply for her position as Queen.

Today, the Princess and her husband are involved in far more engagements than are ever printed in the Court Circular, and blanks in her public diary do not necessarily mean that the Princess and her husband are enjoying free time. Evenings are often spent providing hospitality to those they have met abroad, and who might be making a private visit to England, or even speech-writing. Weekends are a popular time for charities to hold events, and the Ogilvys still sacrifice much of their time to such work, helping when they can. The International Year of the Disabled in 1980, as one close friend has testified, touched and moved Angus in particular, for as a constant sufferer from back trouble which at times restricts his choice of movements, he felt that his own problems were unimportant compared to the suffering of others, and did all he could to help.

When the Ogilvys are not entertaining, their happiest time is with their children. Although Alexandra plays the piano for relaxation when she can, she and her husband have little chance for any hobbies, and prefer to pass the time with their family. James and Marina will not take part in public life, and although it is too early to say what they will do with their lives, it is their parents' hope that they will be involved in some charitable work during part of their spare time. James took part in photography competitions at Eton and won several prizes before leaving in 1981. Like his father, he is a skilled draughtsman. He has inherited the good looks of his parents, and like his sister Marina aged fifteen, is completely unsnobbish about his family. Marina takes more after her mother in interests, and at her school, St Mary's in Wantage, has shown a special gift for music, specializing like Alexandra in the piano. She is also fond of horses, and follows the life of any schoolgirl, completely uncomplicated by any ideas of self-importance.

The self-effacing approach to life represented by James and Marina is, of course, largely due to the influence of their parents' who have been determined that their children should grow up to enjoy as normal a life as possible. There have been no special privileges, and when for example, a chauffeur has to be sent to pick either of the children up from school, the young Ogilvys are happier if he arrives unobtrusively in casual clothing, rather than creating attention by appearing in a uniform.

This refreshing approach which Alexandra has brought to the monarchy cannot have been easy, for it takes many years to bring changes which make royalty understandable in an age which encourages the demolition of class barriers, and which sometimes suggests that the monarchy, as an institution, is an anachronism.

Amongst the royal family, Alexandra has been perhaps unique in recognizing the need for more approachability if the monarchy is to survive, and by her innovations has, in a few years, speeded up a process which might still not have taken place. For this alone, her contribution has been invaluable, but it is above all her warm personality, thoughtfulness, combined with her good looks, which ensure a secure place at the top of the royal 'charts', and a permanent place of affection and love in the hearts of all of us whose lives she has so enriched.

# Index

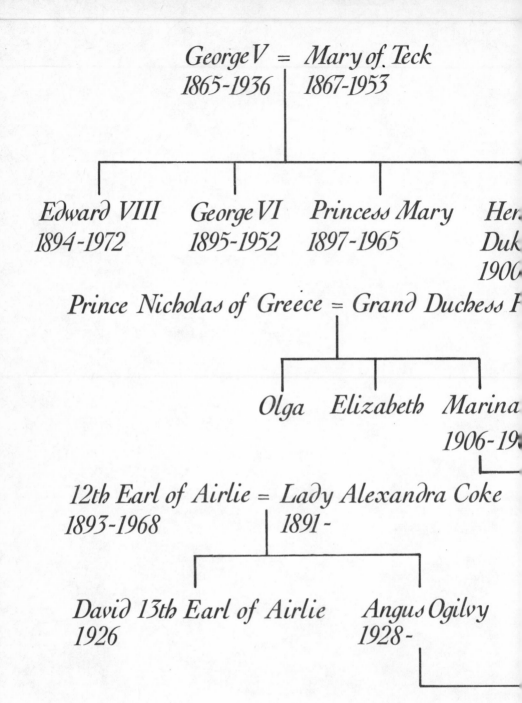

George V = Mary of Teck
1865-1936   1867-1953

Edward VIII    George VI    Princess Mary    Her.
1894-1972      1895-1952    1897-1965        Duk
                                             190(

Prince Nicholas of Greece = Grand Duchess F

Olga    Elizabeth    Marina
                     1906-19(

12th Earl of Airlie = Lady Alexandra Coke
1893-1968             1891 -

David 13th Earl of Airlie    Angus Ogilvy
1926                         1928 -